Obtaining the Pearl

Understanding Your Journey For Truth

Authored By
Joanne Salsbury

ISBN: 0-6155-3692-1
ISBN-13: 9780615536927

TABLE OF CONTENTS

ACKNOWLEDGEMENTS

As with any book written or any life changing experience, there are always acknowledgments to those people who help inspire or assist in achieving the intended goals. Some people remain stable in a person's life and some are transients. Lessons are learned and one moves on to the next chapter. This book was written with the intent to acknowledge every person that goes through changes, good and bad, and if we remain open to the lessons, we will move forward. We will learn to let go and let God guide us through the plan that was set forth before us. It truly is not always an easy process and the stresses of the world make it even more difficult to concentrate on what direction we are to go.

I have attempted to write this in terms that everyone will be able to understand and relate with, as all experiences are inter-related at one point or another. Some people are on a different level of learning and require a hand up once in awhile from those that have already achieved actualization in that area. It seems many have difficulty in accepting help when that may be part of the lesson. We all need each other in some form. The view of the "wrongs" exceeds the view of the "rights" in this world and the difficulty of giving or receiving has become a challenge. The trust levels of humankind have reached a pivot point that requires a look at the real problems of something as simple as truth. We hide behind, manipulate, and control others by sidestepping the real problem and that is being honest with yourself and with others.

I would like to thank Steve R. Kane from the great state of Minnesota for inspiring many of these chapters with a willing understanding of what I was trying to accomplish. He was patient and supportive with my need for quiet contemplation as opposed to going out and enjoying the world. As with my other book, I also need to thank Timothy Thayer, my mentor and guide through my own world of confusion and questions. I give great thanks to Jesus for being there with intuitive understanding of what I needed to know at the time I knew the least.

The world is a great place for adventure and the earth is but a small place to start. Let us make the decision, now, to do our part and change the world by making changes within ourselves first. The rest will follow as we lead.

Other books available: *The Many Faces of Self Esteem*

Website:
<u>www.speakersfortheworld.com</u>

Chapter 1
The World is Your Oyster

The world is the incubating shell for an oyster and we are that oyster delectable to some and not always desired by others. It is a matter of taste. We may be that oyster consumed to satisfy a craving for one person or maybe we are a pearl that has taken time to develop over the years to be admired by many people in the end. In parallel, one individual may gratify us for a moment while others pose no appeal. Maybe we will find the pearl in many people that contribute to the lustre of our own pearl in the end. Everyone needs to keep in mind the most important component for becoming the beautiful pearl: the balance of *Self.* Everyone not in balance, risks producing an era of obsessive self-denial and/or obsessive greed which grabs for that external form of contentment that does not truly exist except for instant gratification. I believe that era has arrived.

Do not deceive yourself into thinking someone will put you or your problems ahead of their problems and "save your day". That is obsessive self-denial.

Most will not be paying attention unless you receive a bill for services rendered or friendly acquaintances need something from you, eluding to possible assistance from them in the future. That assistance never comes. If there is a viewpoint implicit in these pages, the unfortunate state of the world has come to greed or self-denial. What happened to the handshake you could believe in? The trust level of our world has diminished to almost no existence at all.

Some people are overindulging without thought of depleting resources. These people fear not having a slice of the "good life" and they do whatever it takes to get it, right or wrong. They go into debt just "to have." They lie and deceive just "to have". More is never enough for this generation. Survival is an altogether different code of ethics these days. These type of people are both takers and users and usually maintain an illusion of "having" for their family and friends when actually they have nothing. They attach themselves to those who do "have" to keep appearances and do nothing to assist in maintaining that status. When the well runs dry, they move on and blame "the parting of ways" on the person they are leaving. Of course, it would never be their fault! If you are the giver to these types of people and finally stop giving, those "friends" amazingly stop paying special attention because you are now a dried resource for them.

You served a purpose for them, which was a means to their end.

I am not saying you will never find a person who truly loves you unconditionally with all your issues, but finding that pearl amidst all the possible shells is one journey. The pearl of your dreams will be the one speaking to your heart, the one you fell in love with and cherish above all else. You never want to leave them and they do not want to leave you despite the flaws of each! You will assist each other through any crisis, respect each other and insecurity will never be an issue. If someone truly loves you, that person becomes the wind beneath your wings as long as you make the effort to be their wind as well. It is not "all about one person" in a team. I need to add "effort" to that thought because if effort is not present from both, you become a taker or a giver. Together, with loving "effort", you are compatible and "in love".

If you find the right person that aligns nicely with your life, you will feel relief rather than a slow drain of your life. The easiest assessment is to say "No" once in awhile and see if the person accepts your value to set limits. Eventually, the person who rejects your value of living will probably locate some- one else to align with his or her existence. At this point, you could be thankful for this. If you drain life from others or allow others to drain from you, your boundaries are unhealthy. Always set healthy boundaries for your self. Follow through with your belief in them, and others will either understand the belief or not accept it. This does not mean values and boundaries cannot change. Maybe you have a value that is unhealthy and needs changing. Life is a constant evolution. If you choose to be rigid and never change, you may find many people running in and out of your life quickly. The person accepting who you are and what you want for yourself will accept your answer and you will still feel respected, loved, and energized. You also need to respect and accept boundaries healthy for them. I hope the two can align.

We evolve in the world like a pearl growing alone in a shell deep under pounds of water pressure. Until you have achieved self-actualization, which results in becoming a pearl, you will always be in search of approval and constant need of validation until someone obliges. It could be a very long, lonely wait to never for that validation. The pounds of pressure interfering with the receipt of validation include the external world of people and circumstance too busy seeking validation for themselves. Usually this disproportionate need for validation by many will somehow be a detriment to your own *Self* at some point—if you are not paying attention. You lose your own way, your thoughts, your money and sometimes your dignity.

People often have hidden agendas and the ability to identify whether that agenda is good for you is tricky. Some of us need to see a pattern of self-seeking behavior among the glitter of gold and by then, the damage is usually complete. All you can do is chock it up to another experience.

Sometimes you can see right away and other times it takes months or years to see the elusiveness of another person's pattern. Once you get the better of it, you may find yourself with fewer true friends and count more on yourself as a best friend. You begin to weed out all the pseudo friends. You may feel lonely at first, but will feel stronger and more at peace, which is the grounding you need to hear your personal therapist. You can call this therapist "your own person, your intuition, your inner guide, your God." Ultimately, it points back to you.

Who is this therapist you say? The *Self* is our therapist and a representation of our personal identity. It is the element of "I" we became briefly acquainted with at a young age. Our personal therapist gave us permission to play and use our imagination as a component of growing up. We thought we knew and understood who we were and where they headed us until those parents, friends, peers and teachers inaccurately informed us "the Self" was not a developed identity but handed to you. Many of our parents said more than once..."Think my way or the highway" or cross-questioned "Who do you think you are?" Normally, the latter question would be easy to answer, but there was a pre-emptive feeling of danger if we told the truth. I am me.

Our physique was monitored consistently for size, weight, and physical identities with very little focus on developing our thoughts and visions. The combination of both are necessary to manifest distinctiveness of esteem all our own. As children, we are open to becoming the best we are to be with hopeful guidance by the almighty parent we know is perfect! The question exists, however, as to the level of realistic perfection the parent has achieved to guide you. It is, of course, different for everyone. Everyone has inherited some dysfunction and yet there is always a gift in every negative part as well as the positive. Not all parents are good role models, sorry to say, but we still can learn from their mistakes. Do we hang on to the negative dysfunction of our parents/guardians as our own and make this an excuse why we never make it in life? Alternatively, we need to embrace and understand their problems are only a part of our personal history. We have every right to make changes and adjustments for the betterment of all concerned. At the very least, make adjustments in your Self.

Children are subsequently vulnerable to intercepting erroneous perceptions and lifestyles from the example parents demonstrate or through the parents' unexplained directive for a restriction that makes no sense to that child. Lack of any directive enables continued bad behavior. The conclusion of the child has no healthy base of comparison at this time and therefore leads that child to assume if they get by with something it must be ok or if restricted without explanation the parent does not like them. Divorce can magnify either one of these scenarios by an angry ex-spouse or a parent who is afraid the child will like one parent more than the other. Many children cannot conceive why parents split because no one ever gives an honest explanation either out of ignorance or to shield the child from a perceived harmful reality. This is usually because parents have not been honest with themselves, so how can they be honest with the child. The child's soul imprints with an unspoken impression of guilt from exclusion of one or the other parent. This branding continues through to adulthood and becomes that elusive, self-sabotaging fear of abandonment or rejection. What child wants to take sides? What parent would put them in the position of taking sides with an impending perception of rejection from either parent?

Personal feelings and visualization flow unencumbered with no thought of retribution at a young age although the creative imagination and intuition is never lost entirely without the healthy guidance and nurturing. There is a small window of opportunity to perceive and believe *our truth* is authentic. We were truly a firefighter or cowboy and dressed the part with such empowerment and belief of self as a child. Everyone reflected on how cute we looked, but alas, this is not reality. At some point, we are just told it is time to grow up. However, our minds are re-directed to what new developments for our growth? Someone we respect and want to emulate has dropped a ball somewhere and forgot to re-direct the game! They walked away! As Cat Stevens says in a song: *When we begin to talk, we are forced to listen.* What is anyone actually saying though? What are you actually hearing and seeing? Sayings like: *You are to be seen and not heard, you are a big boy now and big boys don't cry; quit being a baby; your invisible friends aren't real.* Are these quotes that teach us how to deal with life in the real world?

These contra indicative statements begin creeping into our precious, formidable minds. To disbelieve in the magic of creativity has disheartened many natural urges children need to be inspired and allow intuition to emerge at the most precious age when it is working at its peak naturally. As we are repetitively alerted, disheartenment is all part of life and growing up. We are told to wake up and smell the roses! Fantasy of dreams does not exist in the real world! I personally know parents who are purposely eliminating every holiday because they do not want their children to believe in a "fallacy". What a terrible shame we take this simple experience of creative mind development from our children.

Perceiving fantasy as truth is valid at that point in life. The passion of those perceived thoughts made all children enjoy life with ecstasy and enthusiasm. Santa Claus, the Easter Bunny, and the Tooth Fairy...all fantastic visualizations we knew were real at the time because presents and candy appeared while we were asleep no less! We did not even have to wait up for them. It had to be magic because we received exactly what we wanted! Who would know this! Some parents were able to maintain the magical elusion of these icons in the eyes of their children, which followed them well into adulthood. Children can visualize and create stories instantly because the flow of thought has no blockage and the filter is not quite in place. As they say, *out of the mouths of babes*. Truth comes tumbling out of their mouths. Lies don't exist at this point, but their ability to create complete fabrications are creative and humorous at best. Adults have a more difficult time creating because they have to deal with doubt, fear and now being an "adult", which replaced spontaneous and fearless childlike action straight from the heart. We begin to live in that hollow shell of darkness, boredom and depression.

Compare us to the oyster or pearl that thrives in a hollow mollusk. Alone and in the dark, its chance to live is slim. It is growing in a constant swirl of water and indeed, change can come in any manner that cannot be anticipated. The oyster's truth is eventual demise that includes no thought or visualization ability to recommend changes. This is not far from our own life journey if we allow it. The pearl, however, can last forever if found and nurtured. It provides joy and beauty. The more pearls, the more ornate its presentation. One pearl alone can also be simply elegant. Unique as we are, whether to stand alone or shine in ornate presentation with others is our choice.

Nevertheless, the mollusk interestingly has a makeup comparable to humans. It has a mouth, heart, intestines, anus, and a mantle for protection. Not all mollusks produce pearls and pearls that do grow in edible oysters are not desirable. It is rare a pearl ever forms in an edible oyster. Go figure. Each produces its own contribution to the world. One existence of a mollusk is to be an aphrodisiac or special treat and the other admired as a beautiful ornate bauble. Both are unique to the same family, but have different significance. In comparison, people also have different paths to travel and yet we come from the same family known as humans.

To understand the birth of a pearl is rather interesting because it parallels a part of our lives we see as an annoyance or irritation, instead of progression. For the pearl it begins with an irritation, an intruding particle or parasite entrapped between the tissue and mantle of the mollusk. In short, to protect its self from this intruder, the mantle produces two materials that cover this intrusion known as nacre. The bigger the irritation, the more nacre used, the bigger the pearl and so forth. The quality of nacre and end result of a quality pearl depends on the quality of the mantle for protection as well as the environment that it "grows". I am sensing a trend that parallels people again. Ummm? Do you feel the same about irritations in your life now?

Sometimes, those nasty little irritations reveal truths we do not want to see or we did not know existed. Sometimes they make you realize change is needed. At times, they just keep coming back as a reminder to look at our self, not others. Ask yourself why something continues to irritate you.

I hope you have built up some protective *nacre* in your life to shield you. Call these coping mechanisms. They moderate stress levels and help divert depressions. It is a behavioral tool, our nacre, which offsets or overcomes adversity, disadvantage, or disability without correcting or eliminating the underlying issue. The intruder or irritation is the birth particle. It remains always as a permanent part of the center. All of our irritations, intrusions, and obstacles remain part of us. It is not meant for us to rid ourselves of our irritations, but to embrace them, understand them and allow them to be the beginning part of our personal development. Our earthly world is the canvass of opportunity for learning to blend irritations and problems with the right environment and cultivate our perfect pearl for the sole chosen purpose unique to our personal growth.

Chapter 2
What is Our Nacre?

Our nacre can be a defense or a coping mechanism. Defense mechanisms are the unconscious counterpart of coping skills. Our nacre is the protective layer we create to keep balance the best we can when we lose direction from our personal center. We try to protect ourselves from unpleasant emotions and usually are not conscious we are doing this. It surfaces as jealousy, fear, nagging, lies, deceit among a few traits. If guarding our emotions is overused, of course, like anything else, it can become a weakness rather than our strength. The escalation of one of the aforementioned traits can be brutal.

Where do we balance it all? There are many types of defense mechanisms. The mind is a powerful tool. It creates our reality. People want to escape from the harsh, cruel world. I see people admitted to the hospital for self induced mind alteration and these habits have become part of their "development" for quite a period of time. New forms of protection, healthy or not, are formed because the past or current way of coping is not working. The physician's job is to weed through this maze of history to find the original issue. This can take time and the information gathered can be astounding. You can only wonder how some people were able to make it as far as they did. Some don't make it. The nacre of their life just did not have any quality protective power.

Medication has become a form of nacre to some. Sometimes genetic issues require manmade adjustments corrected by medications. This may need to be a part of you, like it or not. You may have an imbalance which requires medication, i.e. your body may need outside help to function properly. Medication in itself is not bad, so accept what may be truth for you. Be thankful we have options to increase quality of living. If there is a short circuit in an electrical system, we fix it in order for it to work properly. I do not want to dwell on the use of medications though. That is for the doctors. Again, overuse of anything is not good.

Truth is the highest quality of nacre and sadly a concept few understand. Everyone is scurrying to find "their" way and running into the same environments which enable the continuous need for denial, lies and self medication. We learn to lie if we get by with it, and it becomes part of one's nature. The key now is to know/remember fact from fiction. Someone's story may sound reasonable to us at the time because we did not have an answer for ourselves. Now we are using someone else's nacre of "truth"? Did we check the purity and accuracy of their nacre or just assume it was quality nacre? If we allow others to quote our truths for us, maybe we begin to believe our own lies and justify why we need to lie because we become our own truth, dysfunctional or not.

The hard knocks in life build good nacre if you learn from them. This present generation grew up having it all without need of an internalized "feeling process" necessary to develop protective nacre. They were handed everything, enabled, bailed out and *hence,* now the time of *"not having"* is here and no one knows how to function when things get tough. They stand with their hand out feeling entitled or have a "melt down", as they call it now, if they don't receive what they want. People are also enabling these "melt downs" by giving more external "pacifiers" to temporarily relieve stress of anyone within range. This is not the norm!

We have lost the natural ability to release stress because we have been given things to "divert" us from experiencing the momentary feeling of a negative emotion. If you quit crying, I will buy you something. It may even surpass the bargaining and straight to buying something to keep the tears away. Does this protect you from feeling pain? What happens if you can't buy anything at that moment of stress? A little anxiety erupts?

In order to shield their child from experiencing what they had to experience, parents shield them from societies' plights until it is too late to develop a natural and healthy coping mechanism. People have that "melt down". They can't cope. They feel there is no light at the end of the tunnel. They cannot find the tree which money and "things" grow on. They begin to overindulge in their chosen method in order to become numb to the new pressures. They usually follow the dysfunctional cycle of the parent's choice of coping. Hopelessness prevails. Healthy coping skills are unknown, so lies and deceit becomes the protective shield to keep problems at bay. No one wants to admit they do not know how to make it on their own. Survival becomes a dysfunctional mess. People begin to have your number and that feeling of hopelessness begins to emerge.

One mollusk consistently lives its natural truth by creating a pearl. Sometimes the pearl is plucked before it can grow. The pearl cannot ever control what happens to itself even if completely undisturbed because we all know change is inevitable in any venue of life. Sometimes, the pearl may never be found , but it still grows. No one ever knows of it. It does not mean the pearl doesn't exist because we don't see it right now. The natural process is still occurring.

For humans, we have no excuse as we have the God given ability of choice, free thought, visualization and creativity that actually allows us to make changes in our growth and direction. Yes, we could be plucked before we reach our mature pearl stage; we will hit bumps, have bruised egos, loss of money, loss of friends, relationship changes. It happens to all of us. So, what makes some get through it better than others? Your self esteem is the key. Knowing yourself better than anyone and understanding the need for important healthy coping releases for these unpleasant emotions, experiences and problems is paramount. They are already as much a part of you as is the "intruder" beginning the life of the pearl. It is part of nature's progression. How you utilize your intrusions is still your choice.

oᑘo

Chapter 3
Release vs. Riddance?

You may have just happened onto this book or are just curious about learning. It doesn't matter. It takes only one sentence or thought to ignite desire, make the ultimate change, let go of a non-productive past, which to date, may not have been working for you. We keep trying to rid ourselves of addictions, emotional pain and uncomfortable natural emotions, in general. Denial is avoiding the truth of our emotions so are we therefore denying a natural part of survival? Transference of uncomfortable emotions to physically bad habits is proven to lead you into nothing but trouble. Handling these emotions in a healthy way is the key to balancing your Self and learning how to release these emotions safely is the battle, as I will keep repeating until you are tired of hearing it.

In this society of instant gratification, it becomes difficult to cope, so we gravitate to the quickest method of gratification we can find. And who should be standing there, but someone who wants you to be their accomplice. Misery loves company. You have heard the old saying "Like attracts like". It is so true. If your personal center is lost or you simply never knew it existed, you will attract others whose centers are also lost and so it goes as everyone tumbles down the same hill. You will tumble down that hill until you take control of your life decisions.

You need the tools to approach, learn and take charge of the change. Action, I believe is the only way to solidify it. You can not make changes if you do not know what to change. So, it is going to take some effort to research your past and the resolution to see what truth has become for you. Remember, your truth is what you perceive it to be at the present time. Your truth could change many times and needs to change as you experience and learn. You do not have to do this on your own anymore, but you do have to make the decision to institute change and have the courage to follow through. If you do try and accomplish it on your own, and it is possible, you are going to have to take a good look at your present environment and a harder look at what and who surrounds you. What is under that protective nacre? Is it healthy or distorted?

Let me give you an example. You keep attracting the wrong type of person to you. This is a common example. In the teen age years, it is trial and error and you follow the truth of your heart, sometimes at the expense of losing your best friends. Maybe you were that best friend betrayed. This is a normal growth and learning process towards finding your ultimate truths. Consequences are usually minor at this age even though it feels like a bomb has dropped on you and the world is coming to an end. The problem arises when you may or may not have proper guidance to help discern the lessons and learn to handle the next situation in a healthy manner. Your distorted truth may remain unchanged. You layer bad experience after bad experience with no new insight and continue to make the same mistakes over and over with costs becoming greater as you age. The cycle continues and you keep hoping the next situation will be different. You will keep attracting the same situation until you get it right. If you keep attracting the same situations and there is no new insight into yourself, why would you expect change?

You could learn a more valid way of handling issues that enable a dysfunctional truth to change into a healthy truth. Life will keep bringing this "problem" to you until the lesson is learned. Your irritation or pain is forever part of your educational life history. What are you going to do with it? Are you going to grumble and feel you have been slighted in life or accept that you can make positive changes by learning from past errors? You may or may not have parents who teach you the right or wrong way, but there are other role models within reach. Sometimes, telling the truth makes you a target by those who are afraid to stand tall. They may shrink away from you, talk behind your back, stab you in the back and yet they will secretly wish they could be like you. I know you have heard the saying "They will tear you down to their level". No truer words were ever spoken. The person who can evade these attempts and stand tall, is a person who is on their way to achieving pearl status and a person who has a strong esteem of self.

You start to acquire a layer or two of your own good or bad nacre with every learning lesson. Now remember, the quality of nacre that lacks proper nurturing can't maintain the support you need to withstand the stress of all changes. This depends on the quality of your guidance to date. You may need a helping hand at times. Accept it. For some, this isn't easy, but learning to accept help is another layer of self esteem that builds strength of character. Humbleness. If help comes with a price tag, you may have to weigh the contractual benefits, but it should be win-win at the least. If there is no price tag expected, you have found a person who may already be a pearl. It can be a teacher, a neighbor or a stranger even. I have had acquaintences help me more than close friends. Learn to feel the difference between loving help and manipulative help. Your body will tell you the difference if you listen.

Most parents are not all qualified to be stellar examples of parenthood and if they had any unresolved issues growing up, you probably will acquire wisdom equal to their unresolved issues, if any were resolved at all. It will only reach the level of what they know to teach. Therein lays a big obstacle for you from the starting gate. If they were not taught, what can they teach you? All is not lost though. Remember, that which is learned can be unlearned. So if the learning is unhealthy, we don't rid ourselves of it, but embrace it and make the necessary changes. It has become part of our historical education and we can compare the validity to the new information we find and use.

This is provided in so many ways now. We have books, internet, library, outpatient programs, inpatient programs that provide resources for us. All you have to do is find someone you trust, respect and feel can guide you to where you can relearn. If you choose to remain unchanged, the problems will only become bigger and more expensive as you get older. The consequences begin to affect other parts of your life and this could mean loss of job, family and friends. This can be a disabling, devestation of truth and reality seems impossible to overcome when we can not carry the weight of the cross anymore.

Some of your issues started years ago with your ancestors and was unknowingly passed down through generations. You may not even know that your political opinions came from a great grandfather who didn't like Democrats because his neighbor (a Democrat) shot one of his cows. So, thereafter, he maintained this opinion and passed this judgment down through the lineage. All you inherited at the end of the line is you don't like democrats. What do you truly feel about democrats? Evaluate for yourself.

There is another story about the grandma who made a ritual of cutting both ends off the Thanksgiving ham every time she baked. Everyone assumed this had to do with her method for cooking a wonderfully juicy ham! One day a granddaughter asked why grandma cut off the ends of the ham. No one knew the real answer, so they asked grandma. The grandma said "the reason I cut off the ends of the ham is because the pan is too small". Everyone looked at each other and laughed. Something so simple and was perceived in a completely different reality for years.

Another actual life example is a story told by a 60 year old female which involved a past experience. She was totally unaware this experience had been affecting her present life in a debilitating way. She has always had trouble leaving the house and battled depression since childhood. We talked about some of her history and apparently she was very ill when young. Her parents kept her in the house where she couldn't have friends in for fear it would make her more ill. She looked out the window daily at her friends playing and desired to go out and play. This was back in the day before medicine was so progressive. Fear and ignorance was limiting and incapacitating at times. Well, now she is 60, physically healthy, but continues to feel depressed with no energy to go outside even though her mind has the desire to leave. Due to the fear and limitation her parents started while she was ill, her own thoughts slowly habituated to this subliminal programming. She maintained this "subtle limitation" placed on her which continues to exhibit the same manifestations to date without the physical illness. After identifying these parallels, she realized she was mimicking behavior that was forced upon her at a young age, she immediately understood those rules no longer have to apply. She got up, smiled and gave herself permission to go have fun. So simple sometimes.

Playing it too safe may limit your experiences and without experience you cannot find your ultimate truth. You may simply acquire the distorted truth of the ones who guide you. Some of your issues may not even belong to you as the prior story of the woman who was ill at a young age. It is still part of the history. The journey could actually be quite interesting if you allow it. If there is no historical data for you to access, start with what you know. Identify patterns, triggers, or anything not working for you. What causes you pain or stress? List them on paper. The list will grow and at times change. It should change as you grow. The more you know about yourself, the less people will be able to control your actions, thoughts and truth. I believe Socrates felt strongly about this sentiment as he wrote "To thine own self be true".

Some people have horrible visions to face from their childhood, but understand this is not part of your inborn perfection. This was another's reality forced on you. Yes, it creates a new reality for you when you are at the most vulnerable age of thinking adults have your best interests at heart. Remember, I said most people are in obsessive self denial or over-indulgence due to their own unresolved issues and you are not only carrying the weight of their issues but now your own as well. If familial baggage is carried down through generations, it can be quite a burden to bare by the time it gets to you. Seems unfair, yes, but simply let go and shout it is not your baggage anymore! Sort your baggage from their baggage and focus attentions on yours. You are here to overcome YOUR obstacles, not the problems of everyone in your family from generations ago.

Letting go is fearful to most because they are used to carrying this burden around like a suitcase. The thought of being relieved of this baggage becomes an unknown emptiness even more scary. This becomes our normal way of life and we feel guilty if we dismiss a "friend" or "family" member. It becomes an addiction of loyalty. You do or feel something for so long it becomes part of your learned behavior. Out of loyalty you purchase a burro to carry the load. You will need to be responsible for feeding and keeping it safe because someone has to be responsible. Do you need this responsibility? Will your life be richer by keeping the burro and the baggage? Let go. You are struggling too much to resolve issues which may not be yours. The more you struggle and hold on to everyone's baggage, the heavier it gets for you to carry. Let go.

Chapter 4
How Do You Let Go?

The first thing you need to do is stop listening to other people and their opinions of what you should be doing with your life. The weight of these opinions can be unbearable. This presents a problem when you are young because you are required to abide by the rules of the house and the keeper of the household. This can be unfortunate if it is not a nurturing environment. So, depending on their level of awareness, the level for the pool of information you have to draw positive solutions may be minimal. This sets your life plan for overcoming inherent obstacles. We all have a certain amount of dysfunction because parents can't know everything. We all make mistakes through trial and error.

As it has been said, there are really no wrong decisions, just other decisions. We are not to interfere with a person's decision unless it is a matter of life and death. If someone identifies a choice which could be a harm to themselves or another person, we need to attempt to re-direct that choice if we can. If we are not successful, we are not responsible for the end result. We did all we could to influence that decision.

In normal situations, erroneous decisions that do not cause harm only add to the refinement of future decisions for similar conditions. Insight increases the ability to see a predicament transpiring sooner than later and enables choices that end with an improved result. Your self esteem level will increase with these experiences if you learn from your experiences. The bumps and bruises you get along the way are all part of developing that pearl inside you.

Truth and self esteem go hand in hand. You cannot have self esteem without truth. This is knowing yourself so well that you can set healthy boundaries and no one can move you off your own mark. Your truth is yours and yours alone. It is not your friend's truth, family's truth or teacher's truth. Their truth is information for you to take into consideration and evaluate the validity it has in your life. Facts are facts, but how you interpret the facts is what matters. Every fact can be interpreted differently, depending on a person's perception. Look at the bible. So many religions have emerged out of the same writings. We take perception, add opinion and someone who believes their truth to be the one truth. Now you could have a religion or even a cult.

We have seen what the cult groups manage to accomplish. They take people who have no truth for themselves and give them a truth. This type of living has led large numbers of people to their death because they were told to believe something is a truth and if it sounds appropriate, why not? The leader says this is the way and God wants it this way, so it must be truth. No one wants to sin against God! For your information, God would not expect you to do anything that is deadly.

Let us go back and identify your truths along the way before they became distorted. When you are a baby you are functioning in au natural response mode. You eat, sleep and eliminate. You are helpless to do this on your own without assistance. You count on your caretakers to give you the right food, enough sleep and change you regularly. Easier said than done for many parents. If they are not able to give you the basic quality nurturing, you cry and cry and cry. It is the only way you have to communicate at this age when something is wrong. Depending on the perception of the caretaker and how they were raised, which is usually mimicked, you could lay there and cry, and they may never touch you. *"Let them cry"* they say. Already your distortion is beginning to develop as to intimacy issues and you are not out of diapers yet. You are learning love means no touching, no nurturing and maybe you attach yelling with it. You have no idea what alternative truths are available because you never experienced anything different. So if continued, you eventually will adapt the same or similar response to situations. You will begin to think this is love. You will continue to believe in this exact method of love until you learn what true loving offers if you can ever recognize it. I believe every person experiences true loving at one time but may not embrace it because true loving is a concept that was quickly dismissed as uncomfortable and foreign.

When we are pre-school age we have minds of a creator. We discussed this earlier about wanting to be special for Halloween and your Mom makes or buys you a costume to facilitate being the part you want to play. When you get to a certain age, parents become apprehensive about letting you remain in fantasy, so they shock you by telling you none of it was real. We have to grow up now. You are too big for this. The child is now confused. How long has this lie been going on? What might this be? Is this allowed? My truth was so different and now you are telling me this doesn't exist? I liked who I was becoming and the way I was living. Who said having fun needs to stop? I was happy! Well, who am I now? Who is going to help guide me to that promised land which will continue making me happy?

We tumble into adolescent years. We are ready to try out everything we have learned to date! Our natural delusion at this age is to know all the answers now. No one can be convinced differently at this point without experience. Therein lies the necessary freedom to make decisions, right or wrong, if harm is not part of the equation. If we are not allowed to make decisions or we are "protected" from the cruel world by diversions, the soul accepts this as valid and true because we learned this from our parents. They are my wisdom for what is right or wrong. We learned our parents can also mislead us and get by with it. Let it be said "there is a time and place to fudge the truth" *they say*. Now fudging the truth becomes a "white lie" and the definition of a white lie is perceived justification as a non harmful untruth. It exists to protect someone from truth that could be painful or to conceal behavior which someone may not approve. Ironic? Yes truth can hurt and usually does, but the alternative opens a door to a character flaw which changes how the universe responds. There are filters needed to regulate what one says and when to say it. Maybe that person needs to learn a lesson and your interference could slow their process or occur too soon before they are ready to understand. Let them ask for help when they are ready. Karma can be instant at times in a positive or negative way and will continue to reappear until you do "get it" right or understand. Do unto others as you would hope they do unto you. It could make the growth process less painful.

There is peer pressure from every angle and we have to prove we are valid even if we have to lie to prove it. We think. It all depends on how we were raised to handle peer pressures. If there was no guidance, no structure, no consequences or follow through for our previous behaviors or lies, it would be reasonable to conclude our direction will follow the same path with consequences that become more serious as we approach adulthood. Now we are held more accountable. This accountability may not come from parents but from the law, the bank, a school, or a companion. Accountability? Now what is going to happen? We are becoming adults now. The perception of our reality may be misguided and distorted, but never the less, is real to us. We sit confused, scared and create more lies to cover the original lies. Who is it going to hurt? The one who believes in you, of course. Now you are creating doubt of everything you do or say in their eyes. They begin to question your every move. Ahhh, now they are getting too close! You may be found out, so you run emotionally or even physically away!

Now , we reach young adulthood. We do know everything now! No one can tell us anything more and we are old enough to make decisions for ourselves. If we have learned from our mistakes, we will have a more focused adulthood with the strength and coping skills to handle problems as they manifest.

And problems will materialize. If we have not had the appropriate nurturing and guidance, the chance of repeating the same scene again and again will most likely occur, but now our layers of negative reinforcement are covering over our own ability to make intuitively healthy decisions. We continue to make the same mistakes. We may even start to get depressed because everything doesn't seem to be going our way like we had hoped. We begin to ask ourselves what is wrong and those old tapes of parental voices begin to play. Parents said "You are no good". "You are lazy lazy". "Is this true? Look where I am in life. I didn't ask for this. Maybe my parents are right. Are they right?" Wrong.

Let me tell you, this is a myth. A very few of us may have been blessed with almost perfect parents, but my guess is most of us had parents who are still dealing or have dealt with issues from their childhood and are clueless how their life could possibly affect the way you develop. I don't know how many times I heard parents say they just don't know how their child turned out the way they did and drop them off at the hospital to be fixed. I know some parents need the same educational process as the children. Learning to cope with the fact that your parents are dysfunctional and can't admit it, could make one very angry or very depressed, especially when the parent cannot see what they have done.

Children have such anger built up at an early age now. They feel let down. We may not like the truth we see and feel even more helpless to change it. Yet it is still valid to us until our perception or our environment changes. Remember, you cannot change someone else. You have to change yourself. Their perception is valid to them and you may never change their opinion or behavior. You do have the power to change your opinion and accept they may never change. So if you are enrolled in a program to be "fixed", look at this as a wonderful opportunity to change instead of feeling you are being punished.

Now this way of life becomes part of your personal life history and experience. You still own your thoughts and attitudes and what you believe in. If you do not like what you see right now, you can take steps to change anything you feel no longer has value for you. You deserve the best and you can start by surrounding yourself with those who do have your best interests at heart. Finding these people definitely can be a treasure hunt and the unveiling of those who do not have your best interests can be painful at times. You will know, because your body and sometimes your pocketbook will tell you. You will feel instant relief when the correct decision is made or the right person is trusted. If you feel doubt, uncertainty or a continued stress that gnaws at you, then you can be certain something still needs to be uncovered and removed. Sometimes this may include individuals in your life. Yes, let go of them too.

Your truth will consistently change if you allow yourself to experience and learn. It needs to change. Life is a constant process to find your ultimate truth in the end. Your pearl will grow and become more polished if you nurture yourself, continuing to accept your mistakes, learn from them and recognize impending challenges that may re- occur. You refine and refine until you know you know. No one can push you off your path anymore with their should, ought and musts of opinion. Let go of what doesn't work. Maybe dysfunction is the fantasy that isn't real.

ళ₩ౖ

Chapter 5
Dealing with Disappointments

Disappointments are common and occur when your expectations are not realized. This is not an easy concept to understand, but living life without expectations is much more difficult. I learned many years ago that if you can eliminate expectations you will minimize your disappointments if not eliminate them altogether. This may seem confusing to you because you are trained to have expectation. This is confused with hope. Hope is the general feeling some desire will be fulfilled. Notice the difference in words. Do you expect it to happen without effort and thought or do you know it will be fulfilled if you don't give up. With hope you have a goal, a focus you strive to achieve. Expectation is ordained to occur in your mind regardless of everyone's perceived reality or effort.

As I said in the first chapter, if you wait for someone to do it for you, you may be waiting for a long time for something that never comes. This is where disappointment occurs because we have waited for someone to validate our efforts and make it right for us. That is what our parents did and now everyone else should too, right? Wrong. Parents have not done you any favors by letting you get by with shenanigan behavior. They have only put a nail into your growth and development. The nail being a limitation.

In relationships, we have expectations. Maybe two people have been together for a long time and everything seems to be working right now. When it is right, you will know it. There will be no doubts or questions. You will feel light, content and humor will override any flaws.

It also may take time to recognize and accept this is the right person. Maybe there are hidden issues that one or both need to deal with in order for the relationship to get stronger. I believe correct relationships do not need as much work as everyone says. If you are secure with your self esteem level you will not only attract the person you don't want to change, but they will not want to change you. There is minimal fuss. If you are continually nagging, complaining, and trying to change somebody or you are so disappointed in their performance, of course there will be arguments, breakups and divorces. Respect is necessary from both people. And yes, it will take lots of work to repair. Feelings are fragile. Everyone has the choice to push others hard by insisting on change or focusing on themselves and letting the world change around them. There is no wrong decision in making a choice to be in a specific relationship because hopefully you will learn from any situation and re-adjust how you will live in the next relationship.

Again, you need to look only at yourself. That is your only goal. *Your Self.* Taking action by staring fear in the face to say "I do love you" is a major step in strengthening your protective nacre because if it is not the right match, the other person will probably either run away or tell you they are not on the same page. Now you know where you stand because the truth is visible and not masked. Do you argue about holding on again to a bad situation or let go and make other decisions. You can make other decisions for yourself that may not include that person. Sometimes it hurts but wouldn't you rather live in the truth of the time? Either way, the truth as you perceive it at the time, is your truth.

There is some risk in speaking the truth. Timing is also important. You also have to evaluate for yourself if this is for your highest good or are you making a same decision without learning lessons from past relationships. Do you feel light and free inside or does this person make you feel tight and anxious if you make a wrong move? Do you trust them? Do you respect them? Do they respect you and your bound-aries?

In another venue, your parents may have been a disappointment to you because you are not proud of them or they didn't nurture you. May be they didn't have the money to enable your poor decisions so you actually had to learn whether this was something you ever wanted to experience again. Maybe life is or has been a struggle for them and they were not able to dress you the way others dressed. Maybe you had to suffer the consequences of one night in jail for a de-cision you made to follow your peers' poor decision making. This back-handed, tough love wisdom can be the gift that forms your path in a more produc-tive way rather than having someone save you all the time.

Each situation can manifest feelings of some in-security. Insecurity comes from unlearned or under-developed guidance. The amount of insecurity you feel will probably be equal to the amount of disappoint-ment in your life as well. You feel less than adequate because you were not properly nurtured to handle the situation in a mature and healthy manner. As with the pearl, the environment is most important for growth and the parent who could not give you money and material things possibly, and unknowlingly, gave you wisdom, comfort and love through feeling the pain of "not having". It may seem like back-handed luck (you can't see the value of the "lack of" at the time of your misery) when you are sitting there in a complete funk and no one is able to get you out of the funk. What an opportunity for you to make choices for yourself! If no one else is there to give their opinion, you can evaluate your position, weigh the facts as you see them, and validate all for yourself. Your perception is now in the spotlight. Validation is now coming from you and you do not have to wait for the other person to stroke you because they will probably never gratify you with validation because they need it themselves. They are also waiting for someone to validate them.

Maybe you are unaware of the wisdom you are receiving from yourself. It is all a matter of perception. Perception is actually felt through the senses. If your senses are off stride it is because of a myriad of jumbled thoughts and opinions aimed at you from your family or peers. It gets mixed in with thoughts you do have and then everything starts to swirl around until you are dizzy with doubt and preclusive ideas about what should happen again. All of the actions other people feel you *should be* doing will keep you confused for the rest of your life it you allow it.

Either way, the experience is real to you at that time and what you gain from it is yours and yours alone. Remember this. It is your experience, not someone else's non-experience. Somehow they manage to interpret their non-experience into their opinion and then as a fact. Opinions are not facts. There is nothing wrong in asking someone if this is an opinion or a fact from experiences and ask them to back up the fact for you. Rarely, will anyone be able to back up their opinion with true facts if they never experienced a similar situation. An opinion is merely a statement with no proof to back it up.

You can always validate the worth of the words shared and make adjustments if it feels right to your senses or ignore it and follow your own path until you are able to understand what the words really mean to you. This has actually happened to me. Someone gave me words of wisdom and I chose to ignore them at the time. This is not a right or wrong decision on my part. At the time, it made no sense to me. Years down the road, the light bulb goes on! That is what this person meant! So, do not discount someone's words of wisdom. Place them in the back of your computer bank and wait for the experience to manifest those words into your sense of reality or understanding.

This is epitomized in the movie "Ground Hog Day" with Bill Murray reliving the same day, the same way, over and over. At some point, he gets it... He understands there is an opportunity for him to change things up a bit because no one is standing in his way or knows he is reliving the same day. Originally he is confused by the predictability of repetition that continues day in and day out. Until he starts figuring it out. Since no one else could sense his dilemma he decided to take advantage of knowing the future of the day. He institutes changes for himself to pass the time. He is unaware, that eventually, change will occur in everyone through the changes he makes in himself. This is not unlike the real world. People don't always understand the dilemma you are in and maybe this is by your choice. They will continue to perceive what they see as valid until they start seeing changes in you that say otherwise. They may not see clearly in the beginning, but in the long run the changes will become obvious. The hero in the movie chose to make the changes in himself and in the end everyone around him benefited from the positive, productive changes. He didn't have to change one thing about anyone else.

If you are disappointed about anything, stop and see what you can do to change yourself. This is so simple and yet so difficult. I have to remind myself or be reminded of this on occasion still. I have had "friends" in my life that created so much stress for me because I found out they were lying and betraying my trust over a period of time. They had a smile on their face and continued to take advantage of my good nature to their benefit throughout this time. I received intuitive glances of the lies at times, but could not pinpoint the reality. When I was able to identify the truth, I wanted to shout the obvious "truth" of these lies immediately and uncover their agenda in a way that would have been considered a loss of control. These were people close to me that I thought had my back as a true friend.

I had to strategize the right way to handle this. I also know myself well enough to know I leave no one standing during this loss of restraint because all of my words will be truth, and it will sting. Must be the Scorpio in me. This would have only solved my need to release stress, but it would not have solved the complete problem. My loss of control could cause deference to me and my trust with others as the one who yell's the loudest is usually guilty. This could raise the stress levels of everyone involved and make the problem expand. Who do we believe now? Who is the deserving target? Assess and re-assess until you know what is correct with no hidden truths left to deceive. Maintain integrity in your manner of approach and resolve. Let them deal with their choice of reponse. What goes around, comes around and in the end, the one who maintains integrity for doing the right thing will not harbor guilt. They will be able to let go, grow and move on.

So, I knew I needed to eliminate this identified new stress in a healthy way for me. The situation had gone on long enough and I know I can only change me. My last effort, before I made a final decision on how to handle, was to give this person the opportunity to confess their agenda and I then weighed all aspects of what was fact from my end, past experiences with this person and the truth I felt from other people involved. Did you catch that I said "felt" the truth. This person continues, even to this day, to deny any existence of under-handedness. I knew there was only one correct decision for me as I knew the real truth. I experienced the normal disappointment and grief process because this was a person very close to me. It hurt, but I knew I could not change this person. The situation would repeat itself if I allowed her to stay in my life. She would have gotten by with it. I chose the only decision that made sense to me. The decision was to end the relationship and allow this stress that wasn't even originally mine to extinguish. I knew I had been truthful so I could not see changing that part of me. I value truth. I took the chance of losing everyone involved by dismissing this person, but my peace was more important to me and a need to eradicate myself of this person's manipulative ways.

The importance of truth and the people I cared for had more importance than what was being offered in deceit. If the people involved went to the aid of the person I dismissed, then more power to them. I would have been ridding myself of more than I realized in that case. In the end, my peace returned instantaneously. I believe most people stayed in my corner because I told the truth, I lived my truth and I was the example of my truth.

For those of you who may think this as too harsh a solution, understand this was not a minimal infraction of one incident, but a final straw at the end of many infractions. I had been overlooking the inappropriate behavior for quite awhile because the balance of good appeared to weigh itself out. It seemed. Hindsight could relive the build up of stress occurring in myself and my life was slowly being drained out of me in an ever so subtle manner. Since I am in the psychiatric business I should have seen it coming, but I ignored what was happening. Yes, we are all infallible at some point. I was too busy being the "one this person needed" and it had developed into a very close, but *apparently* superficial relationship. Who doesn't want to be needed? The praise and glory given to me was so boosting! I was like the mother, aunt, sister or best friend rolled into one, I thought. I could have kicked myself for not seeing the double sided friendship surfacing. Instead, I processed it over and over maintaining the same feeling about my decision. Relief. Hopefully I will see the signs of an impending life drainer before I get too far into any similar situation again. I know the test is coming, checking to see if I have learned my lesson!

These people will eventually fill their need with the next unassuming person who believes the facade of innocence and caring. The true meaning of "all that glitters is not gold" is even more valid in this case.

So, disappointments happen to the best of us. You can be disappointed in a job venture that went bad or when someone told you something quite inspiring and yet left out a few truths to keep you on the string. Learning lessons occur and re-occur to see if you need to change or refine anything. When something does go badly, take time to reflect. Identify the evident points needing change. If you have fine tuned your knowledge to the point of seeing distortions sooner than later, then you are on the way in the development of your pearl. Sometimes we have to observe a situation until things become clear enough to us, but the red flags will keep blowing until we do see. Time to accept the winds of change and begin to plan for those changes before the change comes unannounced and you have no time to adjust comfortably.

Chapter 6
What If You Are the Disappointment?

This needs to be a short chapter because if you were paying attention in the previous chapter, you will realize that perception is the only factor that can make you the disappointment. Your perception of your self as felt by yourself is the only valid disappointment. Any disappointments coming from anyone else is not valid to you. That is their problem, not yours.

If we focus only on the disappointment in yourself, this eliminates an awful lot of baggage we do not ever have to solve. So where is this disappointment coming from and why is it sticking to you? Let us evaluate again what is disappointment. The dictionary defines disappointment as dissatisfaction when expectations are not realized. We discussed expectations are not healthy because we try to forecast things without facts or a real goal. We sit back, wait and assume we are on the right track. Hope is having an actual goal, then working toward this goal or desire with the fervor to make it happen. Sometimes work takes us to the eleventh hour or the very last second before our end result manifests. We tend to fall short right before manifestion. We wear out, but in reality, the end of what you think the road may be is actually letting go and letting God take care of the balance. You have prepared and done all you can do. Let Him find the connecting source to make it happen.

If we have an expectation that somehow something will manifest to make it all right, we will create frustration. We may not have parents to bail us out now. They manifested quite a lot for us when we were young. They bailed us out of our predicaments because they may have been in a position to do so. As we have already discussed, this has limited many of you from learning how to solve issues. Your coping skills are limited, but you still have expectation of receiving. You think you are on a track or someone says you are on the right track, but you are not really planning construction of the track. You may not even know where the track is located. So what exactly are we expecting? The more we get frustrated, the more our senses cannot work for us. We become confused, doubt sets in and we begin to panic.

Now, we are in a spiraling down mode of coping with life. All of the "what if's, should of's" are starting to come to the forefront. We start to believe in someone else's opinion, and we listen to their "counsel" of us being a "loser" or "no good". If you add to that any other old adverse tapes played in your historical background, the negativity starts to resurface with its nasty little face. We can not stop it from happening. We begin to feel depressed. We can not find anyone to understand our special situation. We are looking for needed validation and the chances of finding it are very slim, as most people are looking for the same thing. The end result is everyone starts to grab someone else's coat tail in expectation something good will stick. We also discussed we may not be aware of the actual direction of the coat tails we hang from and until we realize it may not be the direction we had planned, valuable time has frittered away. To sit quietly for a moment longer at the beginning of our fear, and ponder the direction best for us, does require calm and patience. Think, however, of the time and anguish you save if you think for yourself!

In order for you to see your unique pearl-like qualities, you need to set yourself aside from others and understand that your disappointment is merely another distraction created by you and your expectations of others. You continue to learn ingredients that make up that superior personal protective covering. Your nacre is evaluated, tested and validated by you alone. You do not have to guess. Disappointment is merely a way to evaluate goals that may not be as clear and / or honest as imagined.

Chapter 7
How Can You Be Honest with Yourself?

If nothing else, you will have the true definition of many words at the end of this book. Honesty first can be defined as: "not inclined to cheat, defraud or deceive, to be without pretense or a false appearance". Take a good hard look at your life and evaluate what may be the false appearance you are conveying to others. Is it harmful? Will your façade have an effect on their trust levels in the future? Sometimes we carry a false appearance for safety reasons and then someone actually makes you feel so safe you begin to allow your truth to emerge. How will they utilize your truth? Can you trust them with your honesty? I believe the key here is feeling safe. This is a key for many issues, but what part of yourself is so timid you may require impartial honesty? Can you handle honesty when someone probes? Are you going to punish yourself for not seeing their truth sooner? Some of us do these very things.

Punishment can come in many forms; Excessive drinking and drugs, uncontrollable promiscuity without positive feelings for yourself or the other person, injuring one's self, sabotaging relationships, stabbing friends in the back to make them feel what you are feeling, depression and any number of issues to protect oneself from past emotions, pain of present emotions, or assuming the future automatically holds a mirror to the past.

Jealousy is a form of dishonesty. It says you do not trust someone. A little jealousy is normal for people in relationships, but if jealousy gets into excessive control stages or needless possessiveness where the other person cannot make a move, then it is too much. Now you have to decide, if you are the one who is jealous all the time, is this person giving you honest reason to be jealous or is it your insecurity? Again, honesty is not easy. It forces your impulses to twist around on the inside until you make a decision how to handle the information. Stop right there. Remember, you cannot change the other person. Ever. Sometimes we may have to lose, but the loss is worth the insanity of holding on.

Try to remember a time when you let go of any one thing you clutched for dear life and felt instant relief when it was finally pried from your fingers. It could have been a bankruptcy. You were holding on to a credit rating already in the toilet because of your mismangement of the beloved credit cards. Obsessive self denial. The expectation is something will certainly happen to set this right again. It worked when I was a child! Once you let go after a bankruptcy, you will need to adjust your habits of spending. Isn't this the reason you needed to file bankruptcy in the first place? If you didn't learn from that mistake, then it will all happen again and again until you learn the lesson. Some may never learn the lesson.

If you never let go of anything, you are carrying baggage not always necessary for you to carry. Some of the baggage, as we have discussed, may not be yours to start with and you are holding onto that as well. Get rid of any baggage that is not yours. I repeat, it is not yours, so you do not have to deal with it. It is difficult to be honest with yourself if you cannot draw the line between your Self and everyone else's self. You cannot be honest about your grandfather's experiences, judgments and opinions because you did not live them. The only proof you have is heresay. So why are you holding on to that sand castle? If you have been in relationships that left your heart crushed, you are imprinting their perception of the relationship to be part of your baggage. You did the best you could with what you knew at the time. Again, I repeat, you did the best you knew how at the time.

❧

Chapter 8
Healing a Broken Heart!

This is a dynamic issue everyone experiences. It is unimaginable anyone escaped a broken heart at some point in their life. There are many who have experienced a broken heart over and over and have built a wall so high and thick, they cannot trust their own judgment let alone trust another living soul with emotions of love again. Love is not supposed to hurt. If it does, it was not love in the beginning. I could end this chapter here because that says it all, but I am sure many need more input into this because it seems more complicated.

We are here to experience the best and the worst of things and it appears the worst of things usually prevail when we are blindsided by people who just don't have a clue that deceit or control isn't love. Love is side-stepped and misrepresented. We know there are different types of love and the level of what is available to you may not be the level you need or understand. We have a tendancy to overlook the "red flags" of non-genuine love which always sport an agenda, knowingly or not, because our need to masquerade may be greater. A non-genuine lover may have specific qualities or things you are able to falsely possess for a time if you provide them with the needs they cannot or will not provide for themselves.

These people are merely the sand particles or the irritant for your pearl development and use "love" only as a means to acquire things on their agenda. They have no interest in your inner beauty or unselfish loving nature. There are those who also try to hide behind the word of God to manipulate you into decisions not otherwise made by yourself. They may insincerely compliment your ego. I believe it is called stroking. Can you tell the difference or know when someone is sincere or not? Are you honest with yourself about the true substance of this person? Do you have a history report on this person? What is their background and what type environment did their values develop ? Remember, I talked about saying "No" to their needy desires once in awhile and see what kind of response you receive. It is the best test for identifying true intentions. They may give you the stiff lower lip or they may tell you to take a hike. They may work on you until resistance to let go wears against your better judgment. All types are vying for that weak part of your character. I only say "weak" if the request causes you to experience a waivering of judgment. This anxiety is exacerbated by their request to "have" and you know it is going against your better judgment. Listen to your body. It will tell you. How many times have you told yourself…"I knew I shouldn't have done that".

These "irritants" are experts at diagnosing your weak spots. They listen to words you say in passing and you live with no thought of how those words will be used against you. For example, "I am new in town and I have no friends yet". Your need for a friendly face makes you unaware of any agenda, but you have now just found a new friend who immediately formulates an agenda for you! Now, let's see, what do you have that this person may want from you and you are willing to give because we are friends now? They may have to give a little to make it appear equal in your mind… like using the word "friendship". Of course we have to know it will be their definition of friendship. I had a "new friend" once and before I knew it, I was the constant sitter for her dog because I had a house and yard. She would leave town more often. I believe I said "no" once and it didn't set well with this new friend. Interesting. Oh well. One new friend again dismissed. A transient learning lesson for me.

This phenomena can occur when you are dating or making a new friend as well. The key here is to discern if you are allowing someone else to destroy and sabotage your protective nacre because you do not have time to be honest about what you truly need or want in life. How important is it to take the time? If you do not take time, you fall right into the hands of the needy and greedy. They start to chip away at your nacre. When you start paying attention to those insincere patterns, you can finally make a conscious choice to dismiss this "friend" or you can ignore it because they are all you have right now and one doesn't have time or energy to make changes. What is the ultimate cost if you continue unchanged? That pseudo trust between "friends" can also blind side you when you least expect. Their conniving methods "to have what you have" slowly and secretly will destroy a support system which has maintained your fortitude of trust and emotional safety for years past. The people who had your back will fade into the background until they see your real truth emerging again. You could be standing all alone at some point wondering where everyone went. You always have the ability to make choices. Hanging on to unhealthy lifestyles can be expensive and if you marry an unhealthy personality, even more expensive. And the cost isn't always in money. You can lose your soul, your esteem, your desires and goals, and your esteem.

This happens to me more times than I care to admit. I am so trusting people have my best interests at heart, I am shocked when I found they were being nice to my face and stabbing me quietly in the back. My intuition eventually figures this out because my radar picks up signals that just don't fit together correctly. When this starts to happen, the untruth gnaws at me until the complete truth reveals itself. I definitely call this a gift and I believe we all have this ability. It requires trust in yourself and standing strong on what you know to be true. Some people wear integrity on their sleeve and others have no integrity. They have polished their effervescent and charismatic personalities to a fine point and made it a career to make even the strongest of characters fall with no guilt.

I have found insincerity always shows its face eventually. It can be bold in its announcement or quite subtle, but if you are in tune to your body's protective energy source, you will sense the insincere feeling as a short circuit in your soul. It then becomes your choice to extricate the source of negative power or give more negative energy to it and allow this magnification to permeate your whole system until you completely shut down. Many of us find ourselves in this frame of mind and do not even know how we got there. It is called poor unassuming boundaries. You are so drained, the climb from the bottom is difficult without some assistance. Hopefully, re-appearance of that true friend shows up to help you out of the hole and assists in regaining your support center.

We talked about the different ways people latch on to fix their own emotions. Some are healthy and some are not. The manner in which you observed stress handled when a child will more likely be the way you handle stress in adulthood. Do you run to drugs and alcohol or exercise? It can manifest in so many ways. Any o'holic manner which becomes a consistent obsessive need means you are doing something too much and now this need becomes a weakness; too much shopping, too much eating and so on. On the flip side, you can also exercise too much and become addicted to restrictive healthy diets. Either addiction is not sensible. This could be a learned pattern of coping that you inherited by example or one hurtful statement from a loved one 20 years ago is still gnawing at you. Someone may have called you "tubby". Now you are obsessed with not being fat.

So what does this all have to do with healing a broken heart? Your heart is still beating and true loving of yourself will allow your center to beat to your own rhythm. Life will feel good, it will feel uplifting and will not drain you of your esteem and productive energy. Love for yourself will not misdirect you into loveless or obsessive addictions or end relationships with harsh criticisms. Know yourself so well that when you hear other perceptions of "how you should be", they roll off your back. Allow yourself to grow from any wrong done to you instead of allowing permanent damage to your soul. Make the new reality part of your personal experience and then let go. The new reality has no more power over you than what you feed it. Let your heart break, but realize you always have control over the healing process.

Chapter 9
What Are You Afraid of Losing?

We have been talking about "letting go". Sometimes we do not even know what we are holding on to so desperately. We become so used to accepting the past as our mirror to the future, we forget to live in the present. When you focus on the negative thought or situation it will manifest into magnified negative thoughts. We are all guilty of feeding negativity at times and sometimes a reminder will occur through physical ailments. You are aware physical ailments are a red flag to what you are thinking? So again, let us take a hard look at the stresses we deal with and determine the worst thing that can happen if we just cut negativity off at the roots. No more power is going to be put into this negative thought or situation.

You may be in the process of losing your house, a relationship or maybe your job. If this is reality and you have done all you can do to make it right, then allow the situation to end in whatever way it needs to and allow the door to close. You will actually feel temporary relief, but have you identified how you got to this point? Yes, another door will open, but do you want it to be the same door with all the negative re-inforcement and attitudes attached?

New opportunities can come if you are available to make changes and reinvent yourself with what makes you happy, not what others feel you should be and do to find happiness. You will hear me say this over and over. It is so easy to allow others to keep us off balance and betray our own true feelings. They will make attempts every day of the week. That obstacle course will always be there. The only way through this course is to make sure you are grounded with your own true and honest feelings. When you speak your truth in a kind and unhurtful way, new solutions will appear that can facilitate a win-win situation. Others will respect your ability to stand your ground with non-demeaning integrity and may even help you manifest your desire. This can be scary and there is always the factor of the unknown. That unknown is why there is a tendency to silence for fear of losing a job, relationship or money. Much has to do with how you present your side and the other person's ability to receive it.

If they cannot receive in the manner of win-win, then you know it is time to make your plans for change. You know you cannot change them, only yourself. You can change your attitude until you make other decisions. You must set the goals and focus on the new goal quietly until you achieve it. I would not recommend quitting a job without a plan and put yourself into a devastating hole with no money coming in. Sometimes it feels as if we cannot go any further but leaving without a plan intensifies the lack of confidence. You could always stay in your situation with a bad attitude until someone makes a decision for you, when you least expect it. Usually they do not hand you a plan for your future with your pink slip. To keep your emotions balanced may require a change of attitude about the horrible job. It is providing a paycheck and your bills are getting paid. That may be all it takes to nurture the new thoughts to come in for new plans.

Letting go does require some trust in the "unknown" and the true agenda which exists in your mind may surprise you. You can not fool your subconscious. You get exactly what you wish. That is why learning to be honest with yourself is the key. If you think you are going to fool yourself, identify changes that need to be made that will produce results you want. Are you playing old tapes or contraindicative statements along with the new ones? For example: I really want this, but I will probably never get it. I need a new car, but no money to buy one. I like this person, but I am sure they won't like me. All contraindicative statements will keep you stuck in the mud spinning your wheels. Make the effort to stop after the positive statement and leave the "buts" out of it. Turn the fear of the unknown into an adventure or a scavenger hunt. What bigger thrill to see what may be around the corner if you keep moving forward instead of backward.

Chapter 10
Has The World Gone Mad?

I have a friend who instills daily in me that the world has actually gone mad! Everywhere you look or drive there are angry people, depressed people, sick people, people who have no direction, people taking advantage of the weak and poor, abusing others, killing others and people who are just going through the motions. What is missing? The lustre of the world nacre is so dulled and damaged by greed and egocentric naysayers who carry signs opposing anything just to oppose it. TV has lost family value or comedic content for the most part and replaced it with bloodshed and violence. The games we are allowing children to play at home are geared toward killing and raping 3 dimensional figures at fingertip. Children cannot go outside to play for fear of getting kidnapped, so parents find alternate ways to entertain children just to get a break from them. Is there a monitor on the alternate way? What happened to home cooking, homework, and healthy family interaction? Anything goes now, including fast food which increases the obesity levels for any age. The health and wealth of the world is totally off balance. All of these facets would make anyone feel the world has gone mad!

I was taught a long time ago for every one minute of negative energy or comments, it takes 10 minutes of positive to balance things out. Based on that story problem, we have a lot to accomplish in balancing things toward the positive. It will be way too overwhelming to have a personal goal to change the whole world. We can make a difference though. What have we learned already from the previous chapters? We can not change others. We can change ourselves. This brings us back to not allowing others to dump their baggage onto our back without our permission. That extra baggage will obviously cause more strain which can make anyone irritable, tired and accusatory.

Try carrying a five pound bag of sugar one mile and see how you feel. Even if you handle the weight, you will probably be annoyed carrying it. Is it your sugar or someone else's sugar? Will you benefit from this sugar? Again, it all depends on what the purpose may be for that bag of sugar. If there is a purpose for that bag of sugar at the end of that mile, you will feel differently about carrying it. You may have to stop and rest, but you have made a firm decision to get the bag to its destination. If someone asked you to pick up this bag of sugar for them and it doesn't interfere with your own needs, by all means, carry it home. If you know your arms cannot carry this sugar because of your own needed list, then you need to let them know this will not work for you. If there is no real purpose for the sugar bought for yourself at the end of the mile, you may not feel so bad about dropping it off halfway and know you can pick up more later. The weight has become a hindrance and priorities take hold. You really don't care what happens to the sugar as you may need the other items more at this time.

As with life, purpose is important. I have seen and talked to many military personnel at our hospital who have been deployed. They say they want to go back to war despite their PTSD symptoms (Post Traumatic Stress Syndrome). PTSD is reliving a horrible experience as if you are right there again. You can see inside their eyes a blankness as they walk the hallways. Their eyes present so differently from those who have never been to war. The eye contact was minimal and downwardly cast. I intuitively felt there was emptiness forced into them by the atrocities seen in this war and I believe I was correct, but I did not discern the correct reason for the blank look in their eyes. I thought they were depressed because they had been to war, but it was quite the opposite for many. They were depressed because they were not still there. Of course, my curiosity obliged me to ask what reason they could offer to justify action that goes against their moral upbringing. They said they have a purpose over there. Freedom is purpose. God is purpose. Fairness is purpose. Love is purpose. Enjoying simple pleasures is purpose. Their country is purpose.

Some escaped their pre-military lives by joining the military. There had been no direction or purpose in civilian life, and they had made some mistakes they didn't know how to fix. It seemed the last saving resort. It becomes a job with purpose and to die as part of that job has a meaning of honor attached. Where is the honor in what the rest of the world is offering? There seems to be very little honor in anything anymore. So we have three things missing from re-balancing the world energy: Honor, Purpose and God.

We have a perception our personal purpose has to have great honor attached to it. We feel our purpose can't be simple and go unnoticed by others. We begin sabotaging ourselves immediately when we reach an age that requires an overview of what we have accomplished in life. I hear people say I have done this and that, but I have nothing to show for it. If you really take an inventory of the many small successes that have occurred to date, you may be surprised to learn someone benefited from your presence in some way. The Law of 250 states that every person knows at least 250 other people and expanding the concept of the Law of 250 further, each one of your contacts knows an additional 250 people. If you believe in the "Law of 250", one person who benefits will benefit 250 more people you may never see. It also works in reverse. If you leave a trail of negativitiy with one person, it vibrates to 250 people directly or indirectly. Look at the world news. Their reports make it quite difficult to see positive when they promote the negative. What type of mood are you in when several people have cut you off on the freeway? Do you realize that your stress travels to others if you are not careful?

Any one link in life is indirectly linked to the many. I always think of the "Borg" network in Star Trek as an interconnected collective. Jean Luc-Picard proved it is possible that drones can escape the collective and become individuals, or exist collectively without forced conformity. So if you feel the world has gone mad, you need only make one person in that collective feel better about themselves in the most sincere and honest of gestures. It will be the beginning of the positive balance needed to counteract all of the negativity that has usurped the world as a whole.

Chapter 11
Honor, Purpose and God

Honor is identifying something about yourself that has specific distinction and sets you apart from others. Purpose is the determination of the intention to be distinctive. God is the ultimate manifestation of the perfect belief and value in yourself added as an ingredient to make it all work together. If we allow those who have no belief in God to extricate this power of manifestation, we are giving up power to be all we can be.

Many of us have expectation that God will manifest for us. Although He is one of the ingredients, he never the less expects action. We have discussed how honesty with ourselves first and foremost will be a deciding factor on what we actually manifest. Your Higher power in whatever form suits you, does know all because it resides in you and you alone. If you try to fool yourself, watch what you manifest. Maybe you want something so much but inside you are harboring doubts. Maybe someone or something diverts your direction. Your true intention and determination may have to be put on hold until more information becomes prevalent. If you do not manifest what you intend at that time, the time is not right for that manifestation or it isn't for your highest good. You may need to learn more or meet someone who will be a catalyst to connect some links. Do not blame "not getting" on God and therefore become a nonbeliever. Ultimately, you are not believing in yourself or your own thoughts and likely are doing nothing to get it.

Many are waiting for the messiah to rescue them from the world gone mad, but the messiah is you, your thoughts, your attitude, your servitude. Your sins are yours and the cross you bare has to come from within to make changes necessary to raise your consciousness. Do not wait for someone else to do it for you. You can find "like" people who will support you because like attracts like. They will not be sabotaging, hurtful or deceiving. Keep moving until you do find them. There will be those who profess to be on the same wavelength, but you will know in time if they emulate words with similar actions. Actions and words need to say the same thing and when they don't, keep moving. Realize if you are deceitful, hurtful and sabotaging, you will reap what you sow until you make the decision to change your ways. People can only handle so much before they move on and you will attract the same people doing the same to you. Take that good look at yourself! This is easy to say and much harder to do. Simple,but never easy!

Since the first interaction of cultures, war and peace have been a part of the human developmental process. There is always an intent for good or evil to prevail and as with any form of life there is a beginning and an end. The opposites do exist in tandem at all times. How we choose to live between the two opposites is the choice we have all been given. If your desire is to serve and protect what is positive and good for yourself, but you maintain behaviors that are learned from a negative path, your original desire for good fortune will remain out of reach until you adjust your behaviors to support what you expect from others and for yourself.

In the future, there will be a shift of energy and chosen people will teach us a new way of coping. We have to be ready and know what is heard is true and correct. We need to practice feeling the right answers through our body. If an answer causes us stress, then the answer requires new direction or is not completely clear. Our purpose is to be and feel the best we can to each other and ourselves. Get to know your body and how it answers for you. Trust the beautiful knowing pearl that resides inside each of us.

❧❧

Chapter 12
What Trail of Energy Is Behind You?

We are all pure energy. Energy is the availability of power. Power is the capability of accomplishing something. Power can end with good or inferior results depending on how you choose to direct the power. You will understand which you are accomplishing by how you feel at the end of each day. If your purpose is directed you will have a much easier time accomplishing your goals. You will feel motivated and ready to start the next day eagerly. If you are jumping around from job to job or relationship to relationship, you will feel off balance and dread getting up the next day. What results are you getting? Are people responding to you well or are doors slamming in your face?

We touched earlier on whether you provide positive energy to others or drain energy away from them. Obviously, it is effortless to drain energy from others because it is easier to place blame on them. When you blame others, you drain their energy and your energy as well because negativity eats any surviving positive energy. As we have said, it takes much more positive energy to overcome the negativity. You latch on because of a present need at the time and unknowingly begin the act of tearing them down to your level if you are not making any effort to improve yourself. Blame combined with expectation of what you insist on may go well beyond the other person's capacity or desire to give if the giving is not received graciously. The end result can be jealousy, anger, frustration, resentment and nagging negative input. This will lead to a slow dissipation of energies until one person decides enough is enough.

Let us take a relationship that starts out with passion and positive energies. We call this the honeymoon phase. All is well. Life seems productive. After the honeymoon subsides, the dysfunction begins to emerge. You may be the one sporting an empty cup when you started in this relationship. You counted on the other person to fill your cup. It could be an issue of money, fear of being alone, dependency or co-dependency based on your needs at the time. The "filler" of your cup only has so much to put into your cup without draining their own cup. If you continue to take from the filler's cup without giving back, eventually they will dry up and collapse if their boundaries are not strong and clear.

This happens to so many of us. The caregivers of the world want to help and feel needed, but the capacity to know when to stop eludes most. They sit and wonder why they have no more energy and yet they keep giving and people keep taking. If not identified early, resentment begins to emerge and, depending on the ability to release these feelings of resentment productively, the relationship could erode. Energy on both sides becomes weak and a lack of tolerance begins to develop. Remember, you cannot change another! If they make no effort in changing themselves, YOU need to make the changes. Of course, they may not like this, but you have to preserve your own energy to survive.

Now, let us say the giver or the "filler" decides to leave the situation. This can occur mentally, physically and financially. The taker's cup quickly becomes depleted because what was in their cup wasn't theirs to start. The taker's cup loses everything and therefore value is lost as well. Now the taker is back to the level before the giver entered the picture. The taker's cup actually has less now because no effort was made to fill their own cup at any time. The initial contents eroded and atrophied.

Fear and anger then take over, in that order, as fear always occurs first. So when you are angry you have to ask yourself what you are fearing. Is it rejection, abandonment, loss of love, death or embarrassment perhaps? These are innate human fears. In reality, you have manifested one of these fears through your own behavior. If you take without any effort to give back, you deplete reserves of the giver and suffer one of the above fears now inherent to your life history. If you are the giver, you gave of yourself for fear of the same. These are two different agendas, but the result will be the same. The boundaries were poor on both sides.

Loss of anything always follows 5 steps of grief. These are denial, anger, bargaining, depression and the goal of acceptance. If we do not take steps to change our environment, or ourselves, we will remain stuck in one of the beginning phases of grief with no capability of making it to the 5th stage of acceptance and moving on. If you choose to remain unchanged, you will never make it to acceptance, and acceptance would actually provide you relief of the stress. If you make positive changes, sleep will be better, eating will be normal, motivation and eventually activity returns, which is necessary to grow.

We talked about the world fixated in obsessive self-denial by engaging in illegal forms of entertainment or substance in order to escape the harsh realities of this world. People conceal the anger and bargaining phases with any substance that numbs and yet when reality does not change, they do more. Finding the appropriate release in order to achieve acceptance of realities is the goal. Numbing yourself into psychotic hysteria is not one of the healthy choices. The release would parallel the fear. Hence, if you have a fear of rejection, your release could be learning to be alone and enjoy your own company. If you feel no one cares, maybe you should start caring. Acceptance is letting go and feeling no more "sting" in your gut when the hurtful past surfaces. We all know the elation of acceptance and the automatic release of anguish. It is such a feeling of freedom and your soul feels lighter and less obstructed.

If the world has gone mad, maybe the world is stuck in one of the 5 energy phases of grief. Our world includes people and people are energy. Therefore, the energy phase you may be stumbling around in could parallel the phase of the mass's (energy), which are also trying to ascertain if anyone may be on a correct road to acceptance. Everyone is following each other. This keeps everyone off balance. Confusion entails because that particular road was not the one for you and/ or them. The right road is your road, so if you do not pave your own way you may never reach acceptance. People who ultimately cannot find their own path push others out of the way in an attempt to get somewhere first. This creates emotions of flared anger and bruised egos. The world needs to achieve acceptance by allowing individuality to emerge with positive support. The world is you and we know you are the only one you can change. So, what do you need to let go of in order to feel the release of stress on a consistent basis, so the world can begin to loosen its grip and let go of the pain as well? It needs to start with you!

The trail of energy you leave behind will continue for a time, so pay attention to what you are saying and doing. Accelerate your thoughts toward the direction you want to achieve. If you choose to continue a path of resistance, you will meet with resistance. Is your ego in your way? If your thoughts are negative, you will reap negative results. This is nothing new, but needs repeating until it makes sense to you.

The pearls of wisdom you receive directly or indirectly may take time before all the dots connect. That is part of the journey. You may be in a position you do not like, but life's lessons take longer if you are not open to learning and allowing your Self to get out of your own way. God only knows I have spent much of my life getting out of my own way and at times, even now I am my own worst enemy. I believe my mother directed the word "stubborn" a few times my way. I usually had to learn the hard way, as I wanted to understand and feel the results for myself. I rarely accepted another's advice or pearls of wisdom on first chance. It was a tough way to learn, but my result was a "knowing" that no one could take from me. So if you sit back and let others tell you how to live your life without testing it out as truth for you, you will be plunged into that whirlpool of confusion for a long time.

The more open you are to listening for those pearls of wisdom and knowing when they have value for you at any future point will help you put the pieces of your puzzle together. Your final puzzle along with every separate piece involved needs to be designed by you and you alone. Obstacles or other people will get in the way of finishing your puzzle because they have a piece they think *should* fit nicely in their opinion. You are already perfect and your puzzle is perfect despite the unusual shape of each piece you choose to cut. You may have to start on different areas of the puzzle at different times because you hit a crossroad or block in one area. You may have to come back to that later. Let go for a while in that area and come back if you still have the desire or need. Maybe you do not want that piece anymore. It no longer fits the new picture you have for yourself! There is nothing wrong with that! Take a chance.

You need to trust in yourself and your ability to dream and visualize the picture of your own puzzle. Know it is not always a straight path or even the same picture since the original inception of thought. That would be boring and no one ever said we could not explore or change things on the way. The puzzle will complete itself nicely as you go. If you maintain integrity in all you do, and your intentions are consistent with healthy values, the picture will remain pure. It will certainly be the correct fuel to ignite the same energy in others.

Chapter 13
Are You Getting in Your Own Way?

At times, we cannot help getting in our own way. One of my mentors observed that I can take a small red flag and turn it into a big red flag. My response was that every red flag is big to me because I never used to see *any* red flags when I was young and boy was that always a revelation! Remembering I learn the hard way, I figure I better be paying attention now because I am tired of hitting those walls! I am still shocked when anyone is untruthful and deceitful. They are supposed to be your best friend? This pattern seems to continue even in my adulthood. I become sensitive to energy that affects me in a negative way no matter how small of a "pinch" it gives me. One can easily get carried away though and turn little problems into big problems using that underdeveloped creative imagination usurped from us at a young age. I told you imagination is not lost! Intuition and imagination can mix a potion quite explosive if not checked early on.

Confronting those red flags as they occur help to distinguish the reality of the true problem. Suppression will only enlarge the problem into a bigger red flag that maybe was not so big to start. You begin to visualize your worst fears, real or not, insecurities begin to manifest all over again and before you know, you are in a jealous rage over something that did not necessarily happen. Then again, you could be right on target! You have to weigh all known data and be mature enough to maintain your integrity when you feel these old behaviors resurfacing. It is horrible to feel jealous and insecure. No one likes to see it in a person either. A little is normal, but when it overextends into non-reality and loss of control, there may be a problem.

On the other hand, if you are a person that likes to play on others' insecurities, shame on you. This, to me, is the worst kind of abuse. Some people are sneaky because they do not want to face responsibilities of growing up. They always want to keep all doors open in case something better comes along. That certainly makes one feel special. Other people are so narcissistic they try to get by with behavior they know may hurt another person, but they do not seem to care. It is all about them. They do not know how to be honest with themselves or care whether they are honest, so they lie and sneak to feel powerful. They feel they can just deny it all and that will be enough! Lies protect them. Who is the crazy one here? Do they truly think no one is going to find out the truth? The truth always comes out! When it does, they act so surprised that the people they hurt are not going to forgive them! They may apologize, albeit weak and irrational or conjure a wrong truth to divert from the real reason! Should that be enough? In addition, to make it more laughable, they do everything they can to win the abused back. Defeat just does not set well, does it? Now it is out in open and everyone knows that a truly dysfunctional person exists.

Lies and control have become a way of life and a form of self-sabotage for the deceiving individual. Who are they actually deceiving? They are deceiving themselves that this works. It is always difficult to pinpoint their truth because you want to believe they are being honest and usually the people on the other end feel crazy for a period. Intuitions may be working, but putting a finger on the truth can be tedious and take patience. There could be much at stake if truth is uncovered or are you making a wrong assumption. I have seen the strongest of people fall from the mental manipulations of the ones who claim to "care for them".

A person needs to decide what is more important at this point. Is having money worth the stress or loss of dignity staying with someone who cannot help themselves or choose not to help themselves? I believe society is beginning to shun those who feel "nothing can touch them". Once exposed, society can make or break futures and it seems people are standing up once again to see justice prevails. Look at Tiger Woods and Arnold Schwarzenegger. Their careers have taken a nosedive because of the magnitude of their lies. Tiger's golf game has never been the same since exposed, but did he consider any of this while he was being a sneak? Now there is a crack in that big ego. The insecurities are taking over.

A person's ego is the organized conscious mediator between reality and the functioning of the person according to their perception and adaptation. I stress "organized and conscious" mediator. Most people know when they have a huge ego. They admit it. They live it. The problem is they perceive this as meaning they are "strong" and maybe untouchable. This is quite the contrary. Usually this ego mask covers major insecurity. The bigger the ego, the bigger the insecurity. If you had parents that made you feel better than others, or put you on a pedestal where everything you did was perfect, you probably have an ego that has a bit of a narcissistic spin to it. If you were coddled and given everything, then you probably sport an attitude of needing to be the center of attention. If you do not get this attention...woe be it to the future person who is not giving attention to you in the amounts you require!

We have discussed that everyone's perception is real to him or her at the time of the perceived notion.

Is the perception correct? Perception could be dysfunctional because of many factors. It could be your truth until circumstances change the reality. Do we want to admit it? We may remain in denial. Some people live in denial. Life entails change so would it not be viable that one's perception may need to change to adapt to a new reality. Sometimes people will not change their perception. They are in their little world of dysfunction and refuse to see other possibilities. You may see the other person's view or maybe a new set of circumstances lay before you as a challenge for change. There are always other possibilities if you allow yourself to be honest about your possible flaws and stubborn ego.

An example from my own life involved career. I moved along a certain path, making good money and living a life that paralleled the typical American way for the area of the country where I was living at the time. Circumstances changed and I moved to an area that was more expensive and wages did not necessarily match up to the cost of living. My ego was determined to maintain the same level with which I was familiar, but reality did not coincide with my ego. Therefore, I had a choice to maintain my same stubborn insistence for same price of living or realize I may need to adjust my thinking and own up to the new adjustment. I turned down good offers simply because the pay was not comparable to what I left. It was inevitable, based on the culture of the new area, (can't fight city hall) that I was going to have to accept this new starting point because no one seemed to be budging off his or her mark. This happens to so many of us at a point in life when it becomes scary to begin again but I refused to let it stop me from living where I wanted to live. After I woke up, I allowed opportunities to come to me. I let the universe pick my way for a while.

We talked about putting our puzzle together and maybe now is time to let go of what was and start on another part of the puzzle. We are not discarding any parts of the puzzle to date, as it is progress in the making. Life hands us opportunities and sometimes we have to start over with faith the new direction will pay the benefits we want if we focus on the new goal. Let go of what has no value to you. Again, do not jump around or end up in that maze lead by others because they may not know where they need to be yet. It is like cutting off the antennas of an ant and they become disoriented as to the direction of home.

Be open to change and know change will usually spawn adjustment of something. If you resist the change, then you are not allowing yourself to grow and the results will remain stagnant with the past. Get out of your own way! You may have a few hit and misses, but the moving is what is important until you settle on the one direction that makes sense to you. If you vacillate in doing nothing, nothing will occur. Connecting to the energies of others may allow the new direction to surface when you least expect it as we are all connected by energy. You may meet someone who has a new interesting direction or a new idea may come out of hardship. When it feels right, put all of your energy into making it happen. Take action. Do not spread your energies out until after you are comfortable the initial direction has solidified.

Ego can be a limitation if you allow it. It is good to have a positive and confident image of yourself, but not to the point you cannot humble yourself to make a change when change is necessary. If you are concerned how others are going to perceive you in your new struggling role with direction, you are not following your path. You are still looking backward instead of forward and allowing others to direct your path. You may be surprised to find how many have had to do the same thing. The successful ones will be the ones who understand it takes time to rebuild the new foundation. There will be sacrifices to start, but if you believe in your new direction, the results will come. It may mean more money, more freedom of your time, and more peace in your soul. You may decide to minimize clutter in your life or move to an area that allows your soul to breathe. What do you want to harvest for yourself as the result? If you try to achieve things you think everyone else perceives you need to achieve, you again are not on a healthy path. You are in your own way.

It requires strength of character to stand-alone. You may hit more walls than most, but do not stop trying to overcome those walls. The energy to achieve comes to a halt when you give up. Fear needs to be set aside and faith needs to be the new replacement. Sometimes we feel trapped by outside circumstances or other people. Do not let the responsibility for others deter the strong feelings you are receiving from the universe. If you take responsibility for yourself, you will be more responsible for others. Try not to ignore those strong impulses that are repetitive and strong. Take one step a day toward your new goal. You may have to keep your day job and work in the evenings or weekends. I am writing this book as I did my first book after work hours at a psychiatric hospital. I feel worn out, so it is a constant challenge to overcome this. I am not even sure how I am going to make this all work, but I have to have faith my direction is in place and I am not going to worry about it until I finish this book. I am trying not to get in my own way before I get too overwhelmed to finish.

I am so lucky that my housemate is respectful and supportive of my energy levels, and I know the universe brought him to me now for this reason. We came together to help each other at a time we both need certain gifts the other has to offer. He has my best interests and I have his best interests at heart. A strong bond of support will enable both of us to achieve new direction. People have tried to interfere with this bond for whatever selfish reason they have, but the power prevails for us, so far. If I allow the negative energy to enter this household and disrupt the flow of productive energy, then I am negligent of my own path. If he chooses to leave then I have to accept the universe will not fail me by providing another environment or person who will help me to finish my goal. In all honesty, I have not much tolerant energy left to handle nonsense. I have to have faith I am to finish this project and begin preparation for the next step in my process. I do not have a complete picture of what the result will be and I have accepted that fact whole-heartedly as I do not want or need a cluttered mind.

My ego has left the building. It left a long time ago. I have been humbled so many times by life, I finally understand what being humble means. Let go and let God. You may have a plan but heaven's plan is stronger and I have found heaven's plan is much better than mine. I have been emancipated from myself so many times I have a private joke with myself. I have to "be blessed" because I certainly forged into situations a normal person would have feared and I always came out unscathed. I did not ever feel fear until after others expressed angst about what I just did.

Follow the repetitive gnawing urges sent to you from heaven and take one small step a day to visualize and make it happen. The norm is 30 minutes a day minimum, so if you amplify even more time you are ahead of the game. Get out of your own way and keep others out of your way if they do not have your best interests at the heart.

❧

Chapter 14
Is Someone Else in Your Way?

If you allow, people will get in your way all of the time. You can also be your own worst enemy, so you do not need others adding to your problems. When you hear from others the *"should, ought and must"* comments about your direction, this is usually a clue that others are getting in the way. If you do not know yourself inside and out, you will be vulnerable to these comments. You will continually doubt yourself and your direction will take detours based on another's opinion.

There is a natural disadvantage when a person under age relies on parents to guide them appropriately because how often does a parent take an honest look at the likes and dislikes of their child? This could actually clue them on what direction of life to focus a child.

Usually, parents have their personal agenda in mind or they have no agenda at all and left to your own devices, your agenda becomes insignificant without any improved input and guidance. People do not realize the impact on everything done and said to a child. The esteem of a child is usually not their own for many years, because they mimic parents or peers. When they reach those teenage years, they spread their dysfunctional wings and try flying on their own, but with someone else's esteem good or bad. If the learning came from someone with low self-esteem, it would be safe to say a person would not grow past the level learned by the teacher. Hence, problems and confusion occur for the person who cannot figure out why "this way" does not work for them. It is because they are not working from their own esteem, but from another's level of reality.

There will be those who will follow the pre-destined course set by parents without too much contradiction and those who cannot wait to leave home because of the dysfunction at home. Both can create opposition. Arguments ensue between parent and child because the child desires to go their own way and parents try to quell anything that does not fit the parents' mold. Children do not realize they are striving to achieve self-esteem at this point, but if not allowed to experience and make mistakes for themselves, they will continue to maintain esteem of another.

Parents do not comprehend that every child needs to find their own way and the best you can do as a parent is watch, listen and learn about your child so you can be a good resource for them when they fall on their face. Moreover, they will likely fall on their face at some point. Trial and error influences any directional growth and is a requirement for growth. The more you try and err, the more you will learn about yourself. This is part of the natural growing process and some parents do not get this. If you hit a few walls, keep going unless it is a matter of life or death.

Intervention in any learning process needs to allow flexible controlled/structured parameters from the teacher, so trial and error is experienced safely and the consequences are not so costly. A parent's response to error needs to be nurturing. "I told you so" is not quite the appropriate message when a child makes a mistake. It would be more beneficial to ask them what they learned or help them understand what they needed to learn. Help them learn to process their own errors.

Not all parenting uses the latter tactic. It is easier to say something is wrong with you or call you names like "stupid" or "lazy". Over a period, this brands into your mind's eye until you start believing the words. You continue to make similar mistakes without any guidance to learn from those mistakes. Mistakes are healthy if you can learn from them. They can be deadly if not addressed appropriately. You keep layering unhealthy nacre around an already existing problem, it grows bigger and bigger and becomes more costly in adult years.

If the learning process to date has not been the best of courses for you, you need to understand your soul always coddles the seed for peace and understanding. The soul can become unrecognizable with so many trepidations, depressions and doubts about what is actually real and good. The peace and understanding is always inside you, but you will need to release the clutter and negative words from other people. This unhealthy nacre envelops the purity of soul, which actually harbors the correct answers for you. People will continue to invite themselves into your decision-making process and intrude with their solutions. Usually this overtly insinuates you are not capable of making a wise decision for yourself.

You may be afraid of success because you have not experienced what success feels like or maybe a parent said you would never make anything of yourself. Those old tapes start playing at the first sign of defeat or rejection. Maybe you did have success, but you frittered it away quickly because the lesson of restraint and planning has not been part of your educational process. You sabotage yourself from ever succeeding without any fore thought of impending life changes. Either way you start to sabotage yourself by looking into the future and expecting the mirror to your past to be there. You start telling yourself and believing the shoe is going to drop right back to the beginning of where a similar expectation was dashed. You start creating situations to encourage failure when you get too close to success because your pattern has previously ended in failure. It develops into a negative affirmation when you allow others to remind you of your failures.

You can learn to make changes in a healthy manner if you allow yourself to stop looking into your past and assume the result of your future will be the same. There will always be someone who reminds you of your past errors and if you allow it to penetrate into and through you, your hole of shame becomes deeper until you cannot find your way out. It becomes so overwhelming; you have not the strength to continue. Hopelessness then becomes a never-ending story creeping up on you until you sink to the bottom. Pull yourself up and say "no more". Time to make changes either way.

You need to re-assure yourself at some point you are your own best guide and take necessary steps to begin learning new things. Think outside your own box. It will be uncomfortable in the beginning but each step forward will make you less afraid because you are starting to put new data into your mind's eye and your unknown factor will become less unknown. You will emerge with new confidence and no one will ever make you feel less than what you can become.

The pearl always has the potential to utilize every intrusion or irritant as a part of development. It will develop into that beautiful pearl if you change your environment, your food and your friends to coincide with the new goal you have in mind for yourself. I will say again, the more you know about yourself, the less control others will have on your new direction and your self-esteem. Your esteem will be yours and you will control the level.

Chapter 15
Fear Creates Blocks to Success

There are times in everyone's life when fear manages to get under your skin and wreak havoc with your nervous system, your thoughts and your rational thinking. It disables your ability to intuitively come up with a solution that keeps you on a path of success. What do we do and how do we manage to overcome the elusive aspect of fear? Some say the devil is attempting to keep us off center so we lose all hope and go to the "other side" of lies and deceit. I suppose this is one way to look at it. It certainly makes sense because it is easier to be fearful than it is hopeful. We mistake the trial and error of our past as the foundation of truth for our future endeavors. Therefore, hope can get lost as well as action. Action stops.

If we understand fear is an emotion, which anticipates impending pain, evil or betrayal, real or imagined, we understand there would be anxious anticipation for the abyss of the unknown. Whom do you count on when you sit alone and wonder what the next step needs to be which could alleviate the

unknown factors? Usually you have yourself to de-
liberate issues and if your own vibration is low from
depleted energy, you can find it quite difficult to mus-
ter enough positive energy to counteract the influence of compounded fears, which have now become
a weighted mound of stress. You now are affecting
those around you who may be doing everything they
can to keep your energies in a high pattern of vibration. Their energy is depleting as well. Do you begin
to sabotage those relationships to prove it all eventually goes south? That is what the past has foretold!
You become contrary and pick fights. Love is tested.

Love runs on a high level of vibration and is a
fast moving energy. If energies deplete for whatever
reason, the ability to catch up to the faster pace di-
minishes. This is when hope becomes lost.

You need to find your center again, quietly and
non-judgmentally because it is not always other people as much as yourself that needs to make the change.
We want other people's input, but this may not be
the best solution for us at the time. It is possible their
input is not intended to help you. They may have insecurities, which unveil their frailties. There is now
concern others will see these frailties and all that has
been will change. Evaluate who may be sincerely re-
linquishing a part of themselves for your success and
extending their hand to help. Weigh this data against

those who say they are helping, but doing nothing to help you. The words contradict the actions or maybe there are no actions, only words. It remains all about them in the end. Are you fearful of losing someone who is not contributing anything anyway? Letting go is not easy, but when a friendship, relationship, or situation has no more to offer in the way of growth, maybe it is time to re-evaluate the value in your life. We have a tendency to hold onto people and things whether it is a positive or negative influence because it is comfortable. We have a tendency to be comfortable being uncomfortable. We want to be loyal to the past.

As you hold on tightly to the past, it keeps you from getting to your future because it slows down your vibration. People who are on the higher, faster frequency will not slow down and wait for long while you sit in your self-made mud hole of the past. If you recall, you originally left a bad situation or asked to leave for a reason. You always had choice and desire to make changes for the better but maybe you did not want to make those changes at that point of your life. The person or situation did not have the correct vibration for you to want change. The next situation or person may appear at the right moment and have the correct vibration. This requires some trust in the new vibrational avenue, which beckons you with love and support. This may be unfamiliar to you if you were not looking for it but now oddly, it feels natural and right. If you chose not to close the door to past, the future door would not have opened. If people could only realize the damage created by holding on to that which needs to be past. Memories are in place for that reason. It is the sum of everything retained. You can choose to let it run your future life or leave it as a stepping-stone from the past.

You alone create the tensions in your own body by fearing the unknown and in turn, this constructs a block within your system. Your balance is off, fear festers to the point it becomes a physical ailment focusing on the weakest spot in your body. It is like having a part of your body fall asleep and the circulation cut off. Letting go and stirring a sleeping limb is initially uncomfortable and scary. You could opt to return to the position in the future and re-experience a sleeping limb all over. This could symbolize preceding patterns in your life that re-occur with no real change of status because it is easier than trying a new position. At first, it will feel awkward to modify your existing position in life and maybe you will feel some emptiness. That emptiness will soon disappear once you realize the content extracted was unhealthy. You can now take care to fill that void with your best interests and desires and not jump back into a similar frying pan to get burnt all over again. I remember when I divorced; my first visit to the grocery was eye-opening. I literally had to concentrate on what I wanted to eat. I had spent so many years thinking about what he wanted. All of a sudden, this became an adventure for me alone! The excitement of retrieving myself again left me amazed that I let something so basic as food to escape my personal desired preferences.

Remember a time when you were happy and how everything you did just fell into place. Even if it did not fall into place, you were able to flow right through it as if the obstacle did not exist. You felt strong and determined. You had no issues because you had either resolved the past or accepted the past is now in the past. You had balance and no one could interfere with this balance. Then when you least expect it, of course, you may be blindsided by another who makes the past re-appear and all those fears begin to resurface. They were wearing a different mask with the same intention. Yes, it is a test. We talked about "the test" of lessons revived out of past mistakes.

Do we truly have the wisdom to find the way back to our center by finally letting go of this re-occurring issue and letting God guide us? At this point, by shear repetitive smacks in the face, you as a rule do not always maintain the energy to stay balanced. You let go out of weakness. You cry, "Not again"! "I thought this was under control". That is OK. Feeling weak and helpless can at times be exactly what is required for change. We hold on so tightly to the past fear, that when it reappears, we constrict all energy flow, intuitions minimize, and we become apprehensive to allow anyone else to enter our space ever again. You start to isolate for a period. When you are in that "giving up" space you eventually begin to allow new experiences to emerge. Now you say to yourself "Why not? What do I have to lose?" The corner you just turned may be the last corner you needed to complete your quest for positive change.

The healing will begin again when you recognize and remember you cannot change anyone but yourself. You need to assist your healing by eating right, getting sleep and minimizing use of those things that may not be so good for your body, mind and spirit. You need to regenerate your energy levels with unobstructed quiet time. Think on yourself. You need to focus on your own goals and keep a steady progression for yourself, despite the pain you may have to endure until the sting of the old fears are gone. Acceptance of not changing others finally sinks in, you are back on your own track stronger, and more assured than before. You will be more alert.

If someone sincerely cares about you, a mutual solution will be win-win and help alleviate some of the unknown insecurities of going back to square one again. The clarification will allow you to trust whether they have your best interests at heart. If someone continues to play on your fears and insecurities e.g. *pushes your buttons* or keeps you from growing because they are not growing, you may need to evaluate the value of that relationship. Words mean nothing if the actions cannot and do not back up the words. Words and actions need to coincide to solidify growth of any relationship. The growth can be painful, but truth comes out of the pain. Therefore, if you communicate honestly and sincerely, there will be less unknown. The truth will insure the block diffuses and again the energy will be flowing in a more non-restrictive manner. If you continue to feel tense and the solution is not resolving itself, you may need to decide if you can walk on the same path together.

The pearl grows its luster alone and, if in the proper environment, will thrive and grow into a quality pearl inclusive of all infractions accumulated. I am not saying you need to be alone to grow into a beautiful pearl, but pay attention to your environment, your friends, your attitudes because if you are not in a positive, productive space with the right people you may as well be alone. You will become that with which you surround yourself and that environment will drag you to its level. There is no courage involved to be one of them. To stand-alone and shine by yourself takes courage.

To be comfortable alone does not mean lacking friends. Being alone may simply take the form of courage, honor, integrity, which is in small supply these days. You will be unique, admired and targeted much of the time by those who have not the strength to make changes or stand "alone". They will poke at you, divert your attentions from your focus, keep you off balance in some way and be naysayers on everything you do. By the time they finish, if you listen and follow, you will be spinning unless you stay centered and foresee what is happening to you. You may follow their advice once or twice until you recognize it is better to make your own decisions for what is best for you.

Ever hear yourself say, "I knew I should have done this my way". You want to kick yourself for listening to them. It just reinforces you are your own best guide. You make sure it does not happen again. Ask yourself if you are afraid of your own decisions. If you can look inward and answer what you can do to transform yourself, the fear quotient will minimize itself. If you look to others for answers, you are opening yourself up to the abyss of the unknown because who knows what is going on in their minds. It is simple, but of course, not easy. Understanding and allowing yourself to see clearly is half the battle. If you close yourself off to seeing truth and assume others have your best interests at heart, you may be in for a surprise. I am sure you have been there already.

They say you can count your best friends on one hand by the time you die and think how many people you come into contact over multiple years. Most people are transients in your life to teach you the good, the bad, and the ugly. The few on the one hand will be there to offer their hand when you are down. This could include a pet. Some people have such an attachment to their animals. The common denominator is both friend and animal offer unconditional love. Abusing this love is atrocious. They provide genuine love, support, friendship, companionship, laughter, purpose and a sense of loyalty. They are always happy to see you. They feel your moods and adjust themselves to give you comfort. You are their world and they will not allow just anyone into that world. They are very discerning and tell you in the subtlest of ways who deserves their attentions as well as yours. You need to pay attention. You have heard that children around age 9 and animals will tell you what is truth. This is so valid.

Facades only create more tensions in the end. Trying to control others by changing them will blow up in your face eventually. You should love them for who they are and they should accept the same with you. If you have a problem with them, discuss it and come to an agreement. If there is not an agreement, you have the choice to decide if they fit in your life. There is no need to keep pushing the square peg into the round hole. Truth, honor and integrity will help attract congruent people to you. Experience and feel what is right and good for you to reach the highest path you can achieve. That is love of your Self. They can choose what path they will be trodding. Those blocks of trepidation that inhibit love and creativity from leaving your center will disappear. We discussed this in chapters 13 and 14. Stand your ground!

Chapter 16
All That Glitters Is Not Gold

We have all heard the saying "all that glitters is not gold" and for a long time even I did not quite understand the true meaning. My first understanding this concept was with a male friend of a roommate I had in college. He was dressed to the tee with starched clothes, shined shoes and styled hair. He had a nice car and a very commanding voice as well. Initially, my perception was that this person "had it together". As time passed, I noticed he was always short of cash or there was an excuse why his credit cards were somewhere else. He asked to borrow my credit card once because his were "locked up somewhere in a safe". I remember my face became visibly contorted and my intuition helped me say my *credit cards were not available.* He then wrote a bad check for my roommate's rent. That is when I hit the roof and blew him out of the water and our house. I later understood his glitter was not gold at all. It looked good, but it was not...

It comes in so many disguises. Many of us have integrity and honesty coming out our pores and we want to believe everyone has our best interests at heart. We are always the first targets though. Believe me, I have had my share of hits and some cost me a pretty penny to dig out from under. Most of the time, I did not see it coming and a few times, I had suspicion but did not follow my intuition. It is a terrible blow to the ego when reality reveals itself as the undercover piece of coal instead of the diamond you envisioned. You just want to climb in bed and give up. The world is full of scam artists making a fast dollar. There are people who want what you have simply because they want to see if they can get it. Most of the times, they do not even want it.

I have had girlfriends go after men I was dating behind my back just to see if they could get them. Even as much as it makes you angry, you really have to look at it as a nice test to see if the partner bites at the bait. If they do, you can give a backhanded thank you to the "friend" that made the wavering occur. They say if it is the right person for you, no one will be able to turn their head toward another.

I would personally send the offending "friend" a brief good bye, as they were obviously not the friend who had your back. How you choose to deal with the one who nibbled at the exciting new activity is up to you. It would depend on what your relationship is with this person and if they were a willing easy mark or seduced by falsehoods. Maybe the grass seemed greener on the other side, and they had no clue crab grass existed. I tend to be more lenient on the one who was unsuspecting than the one who knew exactly what was going on. If they both knew exactly what was going on, the answer would be simple. I would be saying bye to both of them.

Also, be aware of new business ventures that sell you on the value of their program with the colorful and expensive materials you can see and touch. It must all be good! They put some effort into this! The program offers you security or maybe a money back guarantee if you make a purchase. They may need all of your personal information to do this, of course, with a check from you. Even if they do not need a check, they still have all your personal information. Even minimal amounts of money sent add up to large amounts if enough people participate. People use the Internet, the phone, door-to-door sales, or other un-suspecting public methods to profit. People have no scruples when they want to get "it", whatever "it" may include and they can make it glitter just like gold.

Glitter can take the form of a friend, a business, an offer, a religion, a relationship, or anything that confounds you that a quality situation or person exists and now comes to make life wonderful in some way. However, it is actually a façade to get something they want from you. If you are blocked by any fear of "not having" at the time, and struggling to make things happen, you may be more susceptible to the scoundrels who know how to find and prey on you. How do you avoid the scurrilous situations that can cost you money, esteem, or self-respect? At some point, this probably has happened to you as already with me. Experience seems to be your best friend and a clear intuitional rhythm of energy flowing through you. Sometimes, the best we can do is minimize the damage, learn from it and move on.

You have to take the time to research the people and/or company and that is what most of us trusting folk do not do. We believe in the handshake, the smile and the words. If it is important to you, take the time to research all data until you feel changes in your body vibration. If it does not feel right, it probably is not right. It is not coincidence. Your body does not lie.

Chapter 17
Luck vs. Coincidence

Is there a difference? This has been a debatable issue and I would suppose it would depend on your belief system. Luck or "luck of the draw" is a combination of circumstances, events, etc., operating by chance to bring good or ill to a person. Coincidence is a striking occurrence of two or more events at one time apparently by mere chance. Very close definitions. Both take a combination of events to occur for good or ill. Which do you focus on as your directive in life?

I have heard "you make your own luck". Is it luck or coincidence being in the right place at the right time talking to the perfect person to make something happen? As you can see it is debatable no matter which way you look at it.

Let us assume they work hand in hand and it takes one to have the other. Does it make any difference, which is which? Neither will happen if you sit home and do nothing. Both require action. Action is the main ingredient that makes anything happen. You can read every book and article in the world, but if you do not take action and try on what you have learned, it will not do you any good. Yes, you may be able to have an opinion about something because you have data stored upstairs and this makes good conversation, but what can be believed with fact vs. an opinion with no experience to back it up.

You will not meet the right person or situation if you are home in front of the TV or in front of a computer. You need to move! You may not even know which direction to go when you leave the house, just follow your instincts and let them guide. Maybe there is a reason your instincts tell you to turn left instead of go straight. Is it luck you missed the huge accident had you gone straight? Does coincidence exist for a late arrival to the airport causing you to miss a flight that eventually crashed? I believe you can begin to see a force greater than our simple desire to change plans, which could lead us back to a personal perception of luck or coincidence.

If you can make your own luck, what ingredients are involved? It starts with a thought. Thoughts are things. You may have had a thought many years ago about some desire, and possibly, you dismissed the thought as unachievable even though you really desired it. On the other hand, you may have had an actual goal for that desire. Either way, past thought or goal, an unspecified force helps you attain that desire when you may have even dismissed it as unachievable because the desire was so strong. When the desire comes from your heart, your heart will make it happen whether a wish or a conscious goal. You need to feel the passion from your heart and believe all pieces will pull together at some point. The nuance of a little mystery keeps life exciting on how and when it could manifest for you.

If you begin to doubt any of your true heart's desires, it will confuse the system of manifestation. There will always be obstacles that try to damage the desire. You will reach a point where you may feel hope is lost, energy is depleted and begin to self sabotage desires by allowing others to insert negative opinions or inserting your own doubts into the mix. This is when your life begins to take those detours. Maybe these detours are necessary for you to learn one more detail to retrieve hope back and get on track again. In the interim of that detour, you may coincidently meet someone that is your missing ingredient or come across a situation that reignites your desire in a way better than you had ever hoped.

The idea is to keep moving. There will be days you may not be able to get out of bed. Find the strength and go get an ice cream. Get out of the house. Read a book. Go to the beach. Go to the woods. Find a place that makes you appreciate nature's quiet solace and breathe it in. Get away from the crowds. We are all connected and sometimes we need to disconnect from the energy of others to regain our own strength back. There is so much negative energy to overcome from others and, since we cannot control their energy for them, our only other alternative is to control our energy. You can only control yourself and your own environment! Disconnect from "the Borg" long enough to regenerate. When you become a ray of positive energy again, you will begin to make the changes in others without saying a word. They will feel your strength and maybe your own glimmer of hope will return. Is that luck or coincidence?

Chapter 18
Respect Yourself and Others

This is easier to verbalize than living it. Respect is a sense of your own worth and how you value yourself and others. If your ego is in need of validation for any reason, you may say or do things to others you do not realize hurts them or pushes them away. I suppose you can say love hurts, but it is not supposed to hurt. There is a certain growth period with people in love that can cause heartache, but if love is real, it will weather the storm of development, not get worse. Of course, you want and need to be open, sincere and honest and take responsibility for your part. Therefore, I would prefer to say growth hurts, not love.

When you are upset with someone, it is best to say what you are feeling and not immediately throw blame to the other person. Maybe they have no perception of what they did or said causing hurt. Give them opportunity to decide if you are correct in what you perceive. They may have other issues going on in their life. Adding one more issue they cannot solve at that point could cause many unnecessary fire works.

They may be oblivious to their behavior and have no more energy to dole out. Words become short and melancholy. If they only have to deal with what you perceive at that moment rather than a flood of pent up feelings from the past, communication will be less explosive. Communicate initially with a question. "I need to ask you a question about...I perceive this is happening..." It is less threatening and they can confirm, deny or explain what might be in error. Do not close the door to communication.

We all have a tendency to let things build up. Sometimes you may not want to bring up one small issue, but then a few more issues surface and you feel a need to take care of them before you blow and say hurtful things you cannot retract. If you are like me, I do not process quickly at times when dealing with my own emotions, and the obvious question does not surface until the next day or later. By then, I feel it is too late to bring the subject back up because I do not like to dwell on things for long. I truly do want to let things go. Therefore, the next incident occurs and two or three things pop out of my mouth, which I forgot the first time. I guess we will always have something to work on until we pass.

Let us go back to respecting yourself as a person. So many aspects go into this. I used to do an exercise with patients that was interactive and simple but made its point. I had them visualize a person who represented a very best friend to them. I then asked them to identify every attribute of this person they felt made them a best friend. All participated in a complete brainstorming process. In the beginning, words came out easily. (*Patience is a virtue with this exercise, as you want to fill the board.*) The process of finding positive traits becomes more difficult, but as you prompt them to think of more, the words start to flow again. You actually need to prompt them to breakthrough a block they did not know was there. The brain lodges in one place if you let it and will not move out side of the box without the patience for it to work again. Exercise the mind. Do not stop with one or two words. We have a tendency to stop short with much that we do.

At the end of brainstorming, you should have a board full of attributes representing "a very best friend". The perception, at this point, is you have described the perfect friend you would want if you could find this person. However, the objective reverses! The declaration is "you are your very best friend"! "Do you treat yourself with all you have described on this board"? You can feel the energy level shift in the room to complete awe of this enlightenment. This never occurred to them! The discussion is easy afterwards. I guarantee the realization of loving and respecting yourself, as your own best friend becomes an interesting discussion. You want a friend that is respectful to you. Are you respectful of yourself? Do you give your self credit when you do something positive as you would a friend?

You are your own best friend. There is another visualization or auditory process you can use. This works whether you are visual or auditory. Visualize a friend sitting in front of you in a chair with any query for you to answer. Choose a question about your own situation but the question comes from this person you care about sitting in the chair. Make the first questions very simple. What advice would you give this person sitting in the chair before you? This allows you to step away from yourself and your emotions to get an answer. We all know it is easier to see answers for others and not ourselves. Try it. You can ask "what if" or take it to depths you never had courage to go. It is effective. The difficult part is taking your own advice. It can be overwhelming when you first try this as you begin to realize all of the answers are truly in you. What is the block and why is it so difficult to follow through with our own advice?

What do you think is the answer? Ask yourself. We accept other people's answers as our own. Parents have a tendency to tell you what you are thinking. There is a certain amount of this needed in the beginning, but there comes a point when you need to stop telling and allow others to think on their own. You do this by asking questions. You train children to make decisions. It requires them to think. The earlier you start this process, the more it becomes natural for them to answer questions for themselves. It takes patience, trial, error and love to allow this process to work. Our world has become impatient and it is easier to make statements and decisions for others, which may or may not be best for them.

Most of us are already past the child stage and now what do you do? You have to ask yourself the questions. Use the visualization/auditory process. Train yourself not to solicit advice from another in the beginning. You may make an error in your choice, but you will learn from it. You remember Jesus said "I would not fish for them, but teach them to fish". This will slowly help you gain respect for yourself and become more confident with your self as your best friend. The key here is to be patient and trust your inner guide.

Chapter 19
Patience Is Not Easy

Let us be honest. Patience is not effortless and neither is living in the past. Both may require letting go of issues not in our control. We need to evaluate what we can change and what cannot change. Past is past. Past is now part of your history. If you choose to remain in the past, I would presume change is not something you are familiar or comfortable with. The change needs to occur now with preferably positive input so the future can adjust itself accordingly. One wants to insure the past does not negatively re-occur. Therefore, we can narrow our focus to deal with only present and future issues for ourselves. That is a load off! Let others deal with their own issues.

If you review the first chapters, you learned that you are only responsible for your change. Your present decisions and future intention is paramount to decree your success in overcoming the past with positive outcomes. It can be a real struggle to move out of times past but you need to keep striving forward to know there is good waiting for you on the other side. It takes patience. "Making it to the finish line, home base, the end of the road" are all synonymous for continuous forward action until results change and desires manifest.

Others are solely responsible for changes in their present and future; therefore, we do not have to control their present or future truths. We can however, have an effect on their present and future, not their past. You can be an inspiration and motivation. You can be an example. You can be a role model. You could also be the negative force that teaches them what not to do or be. Either way, if you do not have fortitude to recognize positive change takes time, you will relentlessly clutch onto that dysfunctional past because it is familiar and comfortable. Be careful. You may stumble if you are trying to run forward while at the same time glimpsing backwards.

We know patience is a virtue, but what does it really mean to us. It is an admirable quality, but at this time in our fast paced world, difficult to maintain. It is overly optimistic to believe we can be patient all of the time. I give the impression of being a very patient person, but I am not as patient as I appear. I have much commotion inside when I overload. The only way I can remain tolerant is to isolate from others for a period until matters settle and I can face issues all over with a new perspective and approach. If I do not have that regenerative time, issues build up and I ex-

plode through whatever manner is appropriate (or at times not always appropriate).

I know others perceive me as being distant or unsocial at times but this is not really my objective. I know myself well enough to recognize when I need space to regain necessary energy to maintain the "patience of Job." The implication for "patience of Job" comes from the Bible. The main indication is to justify our actions or thoughts by saying "We don't deserve to experience such catastrophic loss", therefore we condemn God, in effect, accusing Him of being unjust. Is it difficult for people to understand all negative incidents occur to teach us? So, is God being a good parent? He is our father. He understands the balance comes with experiencing opposites.

Parents need to teach children to accept the good with the bad to value that a balance exists. You cannot experience love without comparisons of knowing how hate feels. Hate constricts movement, where love is a feeling of freedom. Do we interpret this as a bad thing? I hope not. The natural estimation is when life is good and free flowing, we give God kudos and when life is bad, we stress and give him blame.

I suppose we mirror this attitude with our relationships. We tend to throw blame on others when things are tense or not "our way" and we give kudos to those who appeared to make things easy for us. Do we actually learn if everything always goes our way? We already know with no obstacles, there is no growth. It is easier to falsely accuse without reviewing all the facts to ascertain where change needs to occur or with whom. We begin to stress and finally irritability sets in. We suffocate good judgment to release built up energy. We either hold on to where we think we need to be because the future is not making any sense or we muddle through the "Unknown" which may actually be guiding us to a new and better destination.

Patience is not easy. If you stress about anything, patience cancels out with an abrupt retort unless you take a few deep breaths and think before you act or speak. You need appropriate rest, healthy eating habits and good space for patience to work. You need to empathize where someone else is in their life and allow them to be at that specific juncture as opposed to what you may want or expect from them at the time. They may be abrupt with you, which will hurt your feelings at the time, but hopefully you can process and regain the patience you need to ride out the temporary storm. This is where selfishness and/or selflessness come into play. How needy are you? Do you have the patience to allow someone to get through their issue by giving them space to regenerate (selflessness) or do you need to interrupt their space to get what you need right now (selfishness)?

Sometimes we make decisions or judgments out of fear instead of allowing nature to take it's course. We cannot seem to allow things to unfold and it stifles our ability to function undeterred in day-to-day activities. We may push the other person to make anything happen and accept whatever the fallout may be no matter the result. The anticipated problem usually is never as immense in the end as we conjured up in our imaginations. I am guilty of this. I let my mind take over where facts do not reside yet. I would rather stand there, push, and let the backlash of unknown hit me than run from the wave hoping nothing hits at all.

The issue needs handled immediately rather than letting it fester into a stick of dynamite. This is much more conducive to healthy communication. There are those who will put their head in the sand and avoid that wave because they do not like confrontation. I am not saying which way is correct but letting negative thoughts linger without resolve can create one huge explosion internally or externally. When it starts to eat a person's insides like a gnawing thought, it is time to discard or change something. I refuse to allow anything to affect my inside "calm" for long, so I will push the envelope just to get energy moving in any direction. At times, I have to pray I did not push too much or too often because my patience was thin. Apologies are forthcoming and still can generate opportunity for an exchange of ideas.

How long do you hold onto concerns? I know people who never let anyone or anything go even if their purpose no longer exists. Move on! Those past unproductive memories can create health issues. Everyone has served a purpose in our lives to teach us. Even the most negative experience teaches us if we take the time to review the contribution.

Can you withstand the trial of decision and follow through of who is truly worthy to stay in your life and who goes? Will those friends stand by you in your time of need or will they forsake you until better times. Most people are transients in our lives placed at that moment to guide or teach. When the lesson is over, it is time to let go and accept the end. You could stay in touch of course, but if that lingering unhealthy past affects your future friendships, you are not respecting the future person and their feelings. You cannot fully trust and enjoy the new opportunities with your feet lodged in the past. Allow the past mistakes to refine your integrity. The pearl develops through irritations and agitations, and our lessons, which frequently are agitating, are part of our development.

Your integrity is the single most important attribute and gift you earn for yourself. It is not handed over to you. Shed any skin that has withered and separated from your body. This old skin can include people, places, decisions, and beliefs that have outlived their meaning to you. Growth requires shedding. If you still feel the need to perjure yourself, you are allowing old tapes to control your destiny. You can still hold your head high without lying if you can accept where you are in life and where you are supposed to be at that moment. Integrity means you are unfaltering by others perception of your worth.

Allowing others to dictate your next step because you fear retribution of losing association to a desire or need you still have will certainly make you feel degraded. Do you really need this? Will another door open if this one closes? What is so intriguing about what has been? People can manipulate your truth for their benefit. You make mistakes and conceivably grow from those mistakes. It is not shameful to make mistakes. Your past is part of you, but is not representative of your future unless you hang on to it with a strong grip. Someone should never hold you hostage to your fears because they still have an agenda for you.

Do not wonder why new people exit from your life when you cannot live in the present and appreciate what they have to offer you. No one wants to be compared to your "what ifs" of the past. How much patience do you expect others to have for you if you cannot courageously move on? You may be the best person in the world and do all the right things, but when you are always dialoging about the wonderful past situations or people, it makes the new people feel inadequate and they will wonder why you are with them. They will eventually seek people out who are ready to have a future and make new memories.

Alas, you are now alone and you alone created this futility of friendships. Your past has moved on without you and the present feels you should go back to your past since your fondness for it is apparent. What is more, you stand confused. Your present fondness for the past has eliminated your future and you stand without potential for the old or new.

It all comes back to having patience with your self and treating your self as a best friend worthy of true love and friendships. Your past has prepared you and it will always influence your decisions. Do you need to hold on to all that was past to complete you in the present? File it and move on! The past is not important to anyone but you. The only way the past will intrude on your future is if you let it. Development of your integrity comes from unwavering belief in yourself by accepting every experience that is part of your past whether good or bad.

Where is your integrity? Do you even know what integrity means? It is a strict adherence to an ethical code not changeable by others. It is a completeness of yourself; your beliefs and behaviors unimpaired no matter how hard others have been on you. A quiet humbleness never needs to answer to anyone. It is the epitome of what you represent by example. If you linger in the past, you must doubt your own ethical code of integrity and worthiness. You must not feel complete without the past in hand to make you feel like someone again. Have patience to allow yourself to change into the present perfection of who you already are and the future image of what you want to become. That will make the difference in the world. We all want to make a difference in some way. Let it start with you and be patient. All things happen when the time is right and not when the time is past.

⚜

Chapter 20
Praise and Reward

What is the reward for being patient? Now and again, there is no tangible reward or acknowledgement for your patience. It can cause one to be quite disheartened with people and life. If you were used to getting much reward and praise when young, you will seek the same amount of praise in adulthood equal to the amount you received when young. Not everyone is aware or cares you need this amount of reward and praise. You are usually the only one who notices because you expect people to notice. Alas, they do not see. We discussed what expectations do for you!

Remember in the first chapter, I said many people want more and more is never enough. These people may not realize you are doing something so extraordinarily out of your box just to make their life easier. They expect it to happen because you permit it. It is all about them of course. Alternatively, it would be all about you if you were the needy one. This neediness may be acceptable for a time if one is in transition, but over the long haul if maintained with no effort to balance the scales, it is not healthy for either person. You cannot forget gratitude. That is why too much praise and too much reward from parents can actually damage future emotions of a child as they enter adulthood. If parents used praise and reward to avoid confrontations or rejection from the child, the child will grow up expecting one or the other (praise or reward) or both in great demand (equal to what they received) from whoever is prominent in their life at the time. Age is not a factor. I have seen middle to upper aged individuals who still expect the world to hand them their success. They dream or gamble hoping for a quick resolve. They will not care about gratitude for what they have presently or grateful to the person who may be providing these benefits. Gratitude is a feeling of appreciation for a benefit or gift received or will receive. Is there a price tag attached to every gift? Is your health worth being grateful or do you take that for granted? Is peace and quiet a gift?

Are you one of those people who need the pat on the back at work all the time or want money for every little thing you do? Think about it. You just do not get the message you may not deserve more because you have already been vacuuming the life out of your workplace or your home life and nothing is left to be offered? Life owes you? You do the least amount of work possible and yet you stand there with your hand out waiting for the extra reward. More, more, more is never enough if you assume there is more in the well. Maybe there is more in the well, but people do not like barnacles that do not appreciate the hand that feeds them. Manipulation of emotions to receive more can also be obvious whether you see it or not. The hand will one-day retreat and come out empty if you cannot appreciate some graciousness for what has made your life less stressful or fulfilled. Nobody owes anybody anything, but if graciousness is present, more usually comes even if there is a limitation attached.

You may be so busy looking for more you do not even realize the most important people are subtly retreating into a shell to protect themselves. The mantle surrounding the pearl is hard and course. It is not attractive at all on the outside, but it protects their beautiful pearl growing inside. If you are responsible for creating an environment not conducive for the growth of a high quality pearl, the environment may need to change or will change despite what you want. A true pearl has not a choice in the change of its environment, but humans do have a choice. You may begin to see the unattractive outer shell of someone if you try to damage the pearl of his or her goodness.

Let us backtrack a moment to childhood when parents are attempting to be a good parent. They want to see a smile on the face of their child and often times the loud cries that can reach maximum dimensions are exhausting when the need of the child is prevalent. Due to nerves being on a last thread or situations requiring immediate attention, a parent may attempt anything to turn the cry into a smile. Many times diversion works better than words and is quicker. We buy them something or give them a cookie. Now they understand what works! Children can and will assess your mood and intention, but they could care less if you are tired, hungry or in a position that may be embarrassing. All the better! It is all about their need and in a timely fashion of "Now"! So how much do we give or how much do we sacrifice to teach them some things just will not happen when they want? They do not understand graciousness yet. They understand "having and not having". You need the opposites for graciousness to ever exist in the future.

This has nothing to do with fulfilling basic needs for them to feel safe and secure. Safety and security are paramount and necessary. We are talking about having patience and the knowledge to know where to draw the line for those early "manipulators in training" who attempt to get what they want instantly. Of course, children want everything! Everything is exciting, at least for the moment. Consider Christmas and birthdays when a two-year-old child receives a present. They are excited for about three minutes and off to the side it goes. They may enjoy the box it came in more than the toy itself. Think about it.

How much different is it when we get older? We buy clothes we never wear more than once or grown up toys like a treadmill we use for hanging clothes on. We have become a country of excess and the older we get the more we realize we need to start getting rid of things that have no value. This can include people, places and beliefs as well. We have come full circle in time to regress somewhat back to the child who preferred the box to the toy. Simplicity becomes more of a joy than an embarrassment. This could be why people of resource can be philanthropic. Purchasing "things" no longer has the same fulfillment as watching the faces of souls who are forever grateful for even the smallest gesture of kindness.

So stop and think about how often you praise or reward your children for things that may not deserve praise or reward. Life will have no meaning if there is not some bitter with the sweet. How do you teach your child to know they have done a good job without acknowledgement from another as opposed to expecting acknowledgement from someone who never intends on enabling their childhood fantasy of "want and get now"? It is actually quite simple.

Once a child is into the age of verbalization, you ask how they feel about what they accomplished, whether a fun project as artwork or the opposite end of the pendulum, inappropriate behavior. You have the patience to let them answer without your intrusion of false praise, reward or the opposite extreme reprimand. You may have to wait a time, as children of course, will shrug it off and say *I do not know.* Remember in Chapter 19, we said there might not be immediate reward, if any, for patience, but when dealing with children the reward will come down the future road of adulthood. You may even be dead before they realize the value in what you have taught them. I hope it will not take this long, but it could.

If they can't figure the lesson out the first few times, you ask leading questions to guide them to the right answer. You do not make statements! You shut anyone off when you make a statement no matter the age of any conversationalist. Once they do respond, you may ask if they would do anything differently. Still *ask* the question. Would you rather have someone ask if you felt angry or would you rather have someone assume you were being stupid and imply it? You obviously would want the option to identify your own feelings and behavior, would you not?

People stuff anger to use later when someone constantly ridicules and makes assuming statements. The cannon ball blows out of the cannon when the last straw is broken. Conversely, constant praise and reward can also make someone less gracious and more demanding because anger will surface if the praise and reward are not consistently there. The value of letting a child feel and think for themselves will enhance their self esteem level and build a solid ground for them to succeed through any obstacle that comes their way. They do not have to sit and wait for someone to pat them on the back to move on. As we have said already, that day may never come. For those needing constant feedback, anger and resentment quietly builds until the pressure causes an explosion and we begin to feel sorry for ourselves. We stay depressed until the next person with praise and reward comes along to pick us up again. How long do you want to be dependent on others for your feel good? How exhausting.

Depending on the situation, you offer guidance through questions with an ending compliment on how they process the situation. You may have them put their thoughts on paper if they can write. Some children learn by visual methods while others are auditory and need to hear things. The point is you do not force answers from them. You do not issue praise or reward to get them to speak or reprimand them for not speaking. Until you have an answer from them acknowledging their own thoughts and feelings of right and wrong first, listening in silence and patience to be silent are necessary. This is where the compliment comes in. "I am glad you understand the

143

importance of this and I am proud you processed this on your own." "How do you feel about your answer?"

The first few times extended patience will be needed, but as anything, once taught, the rest gets easier. Your unsolicited offerings to effect a smile or speeding through "a lesson" because you have something pressing to do will bite you later when you can't control your child's needy behavior. You subliminally may be teaching them to expect reward for less than appropriate behavior or expect praise because they never had to discern the difference of good behavior or efforts. Your goal as a parent is to teach them to think and feel for themselves. You cannot expect them to know anything if you are speaking for them and handing them everything for no reason than to keep them "happy and content and out of your hair". What happens when you run out of things or money? They will become bored, angry and disrespectful. How did this happen you ask? We gave them everything and now they expect it.

Learn to ask questions and listen. You can read the *Art of Negotiation* if you want to review the method of listening and asking questions. Listen to yourself when you are having a conversation with someone. Are you listening to what they have to say or is the conversation all about you? Make it a skill to listen and hear what others have to say. It is still distinctive in negotiating practices and remains a skill, which needs patience, practice and dedication to the goal. Would it be better to teach a child to cope in a fit of anger or lavish them with gifts and reward for their bad behavior?

When patients get out of control at the hospital, we train staff to say nothing and ask questions. Only one person talks at a time and conversation is directed at the person in crisis. It is proven, that when many are trying to talk at once to this person, who is not presently rational for whatever reason, the one in crisis cannot hear and it fuels their anger. Silence is the best method for calming a situation. This is an example of *less can be more*. Anger is fueled and it is a skill to maintain balance in the midst of chaos. This requires a parent to also learn the skill because a natural reaction is to give in for sake of sanity. Giving in to bad behavior will promote bad behaviors in the future and you will sit there and wonder how this child became so ungrateful?

Chapter 21
Dealing with Anger

Anger is a natural emotion. How we deal with it is the key. I believe most expect this particular emotion to be subdued or even hidden away and anything else shows lack of control. People make every attempt to alleviate anger from their life. Anger destroys! Yes, it can, but it can also enable you to release the pressure of worries, fears and doubts. Should we eliminate love or happiness from our lives? Anger is as natural an emotion as love and happiness. Balance is so important and without anger we have reduced our avenues of release when something we do not care for occurs. It is human nature to discern and have an opinion. Our perceptions are ours and no one implied every person's perception needs to correspond. We think ideally if love and happiness were all that existed, life would be perfect. By abolishing all of the oppositional natural emotions, we would be abolishing opinions, personalities and life directions that make us unique.

Anger can hurt, but so can love. There has always been a fine line between the two. If we dissect anger, we have to take a few steps back. Before anger can occur, two other emotions precede anger. Anger occurs so quickly we do not even realize we have passed through two other emotions to get there.

Fear and hurt are easily overlooked. Fear is the initiating emotion that triggers hurt and anger comes in to protect us from what we perceive may hurt us. If we back track from anger, we can suppose something hurt us and fear triggered the hurt. Usually, a fear of rejection, abandonment or fear of the unknown hits the top three fears. If one can examine the last anger outburst of a recent situation, attempt to track it back through hurt and then again back to one of the basic fears. Does it compute? I believe you will find it does if you are honest with yourself. Fury can appear so quickly. Anger is that innate feeling of displeasure or hostility toward a triggering source. Depending on the extent it affected your present basic values or perceived truths will be to the level your anger can escalate to when aroused.

Anger can be a healthy liberation from worry and fear but anything utilized too much becomes a weakness. Lingering anger will begin to fester and eat away at your physical body. The weakest part of your physique will be where the stress attacks. If anger layers into your system year after year without an appropriate release valve, the outcome will have an effect on your outward appearance and health in a serious way not excluding death.

Society, in general, has so much generational anger already layered into their life. There have been "gurus" offering assistance to our life problems specifically in the last 50 years, and somewhere along the line, we have lost basic understanding of the simplest emotions and appropriate reactions to these emotions. We have a tendency to believe results of a study recently completed or a news flash about a recently discovered truth. I have always laughed at the "news flash" of newly discovered "truths" that surface and re-surface later as an opposite truth. Everybody followed it full circle to be on the correct track with the exact information and never realize they are doing just that; following.

An example of this would be eggs. First, they are good for you. Then eggs are not healthy for you due to spikes in cholesterol levels. Then it swings back to moderation being good. Another example could be how to discipline your child. "They" say you can train your children by never laying a hand on them. Now this philosophy leans so far the other way a parent is afraid to discipline their child for fear of abuse accusations. And who are "they"? Granted, there needs to be monitoring where there might be abuse of a child or adult, but many of us who were spanked don't feel scarred for life. This method worked at the time.

I am not saying it is the right way, but the method worked for many of us. So, what is correct?

What is your common sense answer? Good judgment of the situation, maintaining balance and knowing how and why you are responding a certain way with healthy self-control is all-apparent. You obviously, do not physically hurt anyone, which would require medical attention or to the extreme, death, because of your lack of self-control. You need to understand what your goal or end result needs to be e.g. accomplishing a positive outcome that is win-win. You are never to demean anyone or make them feel their thoughts are invalid.

Yes, there are ways to handle children without laying a hand on them, but it takes time, the patience of Job and knowledge of coaching rather than forcing them to be a certain way because you said so. Simple, but it certainly is not an easy task.

As a parent or as an adult, you first have to acknowledge your own anger issues and how you respond when you get angry. Many have not learned to cope with anger because somewhere along the line reacting to someone's anger might have created fear of retribution or simply avoidance of abuse again. Maybe we began to mimic uncontrolled anger of a parent who was drunk all the time. We learned this was a way to cope and make people jump.

Process groups in a hospital setting or support groups in the community promote finding other ways: "channel your anger into productive directions, let it roll off your back; communicate with the person, exercise". These all have validity but more as a means to express and release anger, not eliminate and ignore it. You can physically exercise the intensity of anger away, but are you thinking how to deal with the irritation once you are in a more calm state or are you suppressing it for fear of saying anything that may cause dissention? What did the person really trigger in you? What are you afraid to face? Suppressed anger can manifest into control issues. If you are fearful of controlling others you may take it out on yourself and control eating levels right into a disorder. You attempt to control your image or what you think your image represents. You may develop "ticks" that show outwardly as an habitual body quirk.

This layered level of suppressed and forgotten anger throughout past years has grown to such proportions generationally, it now emanates automatically through to our children where it starts to bubble as a blind spot. The boiling point is yet to come. The normal pressures of growing up produce levels already intense for young minds to handle. They do not want to feel anymore. They sit in front of a computer because it is easy and interaction is controlled. If you begin with historical anger passed down through the family, normal peer development, add divorce of parents, drugs, world chaos and negative news reports it becomes too much for even adults. People act out in whatever method allows them to feel without pain. They become unfeeling or make every attempt to anesthetize feeling. It can end in a suicidal or homicidal incident because there is no understanding the need for a release valve. It bubbles to boiling over time and ultimately creates the explosion.

Parents are not taking the time or may have no knowledge of how to release anger on their own, so it is difficult to teach. Adults become impatient and needy because of the fast paced world of electronics and computers, so processing with children is foreign and just takes too much time! Any parent who actively participates in their child's mental growth as well as physical growth can laugh and enjoy the attempts young children make in wiggling out of trouble. As the child gets older, the attempts can become more dangerous and expensive if past trials are unattended. Anger grows from both sides and if not handled appropriately will jettison into a possible myriad of end results already discussed. Believe that patience is the highest virtue and not easily maintained. Everyone needs to have a release by setting time aside for fun and relaxation. It recharges and calms you.

I shudder when children come into our hospital and parents honestly have no clue why their children are in turmoil. Parents have no idea how the child got that way and hand them over for us to fix. I have said this before. Even adults need to understand their responsibility and accept the truth of his or her issues and realize what can transfer to a child without awareness of the fallout to come.

My observation over the years points to the largest majority of child problems coming from inexperienced parental guidance. I heard a newsperson interview a parent whose child had committed a serious crime. I heard comments "He was a good boy, never did drugs, stayed to himself, quiet..." Is this normal? Apparently to this parent, these traits were normal. The quiet ones are difficult to detect because they stay under the radar. No news is good news, right? This can be an erroneous belief. Children are very vulnerable to suppressed anger inclusive of peers constantly poking fun at school or a statement from a parent, which insinuates not meeting the same standards as a sibling. The list could go on.

Normally, children will work your last nerve until you snap; if you let them. At least some are expressing themselves. Children can internalize every little thing and magnify their own perception of what reality has become if release and process never occur. Normal rivalry sustained with siblings and peers in the early years of growth is apparent, but how the parent guides them through that rivalry is key. If parents do not take the time to process the right and wrong of these behaviors, one sibling may carry a damaged perception of the situation into adulthood.

As a parent, you need to stand your ground and take time to process firmly with love until the lesson is learned and understood. My brothers used to torment me and at times it was deserved. The process of settling the dilemmas did not always seem fair to me. The one thing my mother did say that made sense apparently to all three of us is "I will not allow you to fight. You only have each other in the end. Your family is your support system when no one else is there." A parent allowing children to make hurtful statements and destroy meaningful property to me to get even lends to conceptual inadequacies of our worth, which is halting interaction for growth. Asking questions and empowering all toward the appropriate win-win result would be more beneficial. My brothers and I have never fought since.

Remember what feelings surfaced when we first began learning to ride that two-wheeler bike. Children all have fear, anxiety, excitement all bundled together in the beginning. They may say things like "I can't do this" or " I am afraid" in a worried tone. We, as a guardian, have a choice how we handle this. One way, you can say, "You don't have to try if you don't want" and subliminally teach them fear limits. They will learn not to follow through with the difficult things in life. Check if you are this type parent, as you may have a strong personal fear of rejection from the child yourself rather than the courage to help them overcome and achieve the scary things in life. Maybe you simply do not want to make the time. Either way you have now empowered them to sit back and never experience life.

You can also say, "If you don't learn to ride today, it is your problem because I don't have time to sit here while you whine like a baby". Ouch! What message does this send? The child may think "I am an idiot if I don't do it right the first or second time". This creates anxiety leading to failure, a feeling of insignificance by absorbing a poorly reinforced response into their psyche before they even begin to learn. The essence of being a disappointment to a parent is devastating to a child. They will forever attempt to please a parent for approval and the worst part is the parent may never give the approval. In the end, they will begin to feel the parent does not love them because they do not live up to any expectation of success. So why try anything? I am sure I will fail anyway!

Protecting the heart from rejection of a parent's lack of love will initiate an "acting out response" either in a suppressed quiet manner or in blatant active trouble making. Any attention is better than no attention! Both are a form of acting out. If this is layered repeatedly, day-by-day, years passing, any person can build up anger to points of explosion because a release valve was never identified, acknowledged or processed out in a healthy way. How have you programmed your child or how have you allowed them to express their anger? You need to ask yourself if someone programmed you appropriately or are you passing the dysfunctional method of response on to your child.

My choice: be prepared to take as long as it takes and insure you carve out uninterrupted time because everyone learns differently and at a different pace. The child will feel you are cheering their success and offering most wanted undivided attention, which a child craves. Do not ever compare your children. Do not ignore your child's request for positive attention when they are young. This does not mean give them everything! This means take time to teach them. The more you can give in the beginning, the less you will need in the end. The interactive bonding that occurs between a child and parent enables a child to not only become secure as an adult, but also offer security to those they love in the future. Each child is unique to the world. Allow each to learn at their own pace. This requires consistent patience and self-control.

Ask them *when* they want to learn to ride a bike. Do not ask them *if* they want to learn to ride. You are already leading them into the abyss of failure. They may defy all prods and say they do not want to learn. (*And some do resist out of fear*). Their fears may stand firm with every gently prodded question or statement you offer. You may even attempt bribery. Bribery will get you into trouble later because it will be an anticipated solution for every new situation. Do you leave it alone and give up? NO! You acknowledge and validate their fear; you offer undivided assistance and attention in overcoming that fear. Once they learn, they can always decide if they want to continue riding or make the choice to stop. Now you have provided them a choice. You can offer this as a result to their success. They will always make wiser decisions as long as they experience both sides and choose on their own. Experience will establish their ability to choose decisions based on fact, not opinion.

The child will feel you care enough to teach them and we all know overcoming resistance successfully is a wonderful feeling! Resistance to learn for future events will begin to fade away. Expectation of learning becomes easier and easier once you get over those first hurdles of fear because now you have instilled confidence in the child with patience to learn for themselves. They will be more eager to try new things and will have a much easier time as an adult in taking risks with a healthy attitude. Let them know you are taking time to get it right and if they do not get it the first day, the next day or week is available until they do get it. This frees up any jitters to perform immediately and reduces frustration for not achieving the goal in a timely fashion. A person will attempt new adventures because that fear of failing never existed as an option.

My mother served shrimp once for dinner and I turned my nose up to eating it. She said I needed to try one shrimp at least and if I did not like it, she would not force me to eat shrimp again. Therefore, I put one shrimp on my plate and assuming I would not like shrimp, gave the rest of my portion to my brother before tasting the one on my plate. I ate the one shrimp and loved it but alas, I was not able to retrieve my portion back. Lesson learned. Trying new things develops your self-esteem level because you begin to learn what you like and dislike. The people who know more about themselves will feel more confident. I now know shrimp is a delicacy for me and I will not turn it down ever again!

Anger can occur more if you never experience new situations. Resentment can set in and you begin to feel sorry for yourself and hate those who limited you. One will never have to be a follower or feel embarrassed because experiences have been limited. It is never too late to initiate experiencing life and facing fears. Others may have had their own reasons for setting limits, right or wrong. They could not help what they believed at the time. Give the unknown a go and see where it leads you. The combination of new experiences could lead to an interesting lifestyle you never imagined!

Anger has so many levels. We do not always know which level it originally emanates from. When you blow at even the smallest of issues, (*The straw that broke the camel's back*) you focus on every small detail that hid away for years. This does release the emotion eventually but the magnitude of exploding can obviously do irreparable damage. It is unbelievable how past memories can resurface into a completely new situation and continue to create the same results. This is not a healthy form of release because anger is wild if not understood and controlled. It always hurts someone.

Those that hide from anger and confrontation are usually identified with their head in the sand and do not want to know what is wrong. They let people run over them without any signal of standing behind someone who may be trying to do the "right thing". People manipulate them easily; they accept less in life, and can be a person who just never learns because it is scary and may hurt. They are marked as uncaring, weak, or just plain stupid. If they ignore the problem, maybe it will go away. It may go away, but the person who feels betrayed may go with it and then you hold on to the "what if" I had done this...guilt sets in and you feel unworthy consciously and subconsciously. Anger starts to brew.

Of course, consistent and timely verbalizing is the best form of release if you can control how you express anger and be consistent with discussing a difference in perception as situations occur. This is a challenging way because you might not perceive a topic needing increased clarity at this instant, so you let it slide until a pattern emerges and see it is affecting you. Knowing yourself and what is important will help identify the need to express more readily. You may not realize how important something is until it takes a contradictory stance against a value or belief or someone disappears and you realize the value they had to you. It now becomes part of your new truth.

A person needs a non-threatening, safe environment for any confrontation to be resolved successfully. Maybe they or you have angers or insecurities unknown to the other and may not want them identified right now. The safety of the situation is not yet established and the fear is someone may leave or be asked to leave. This is an unknown factor in every new association. So how do you proceed? You proceed the same way you would in a safe environment, which falls on you to understand your own safety zone. If your self-esteem is solid and you know yourself, it does not matter who comes into your life and creates a wave. You will handle it as calmly as possible, identify your boundaries, and unless they can persuade you that your boundaries need changed (which they might need changing), they can accept it or they can leave. You are comfortable with either decision. Ultimately, you need an environment where your safety zone is respected, and the other person feels their safety zone is respected. Together, any issue can be resolved.

If you feel hostage to your emotions and your environment because you are not being heard, an explosion of those unheard emotions can come out in so many detrimental ways.

There will be those people who may never appear to respect you at any point because all they can recognize is what they get from you. These are the bullies, the naysayers, the high egotistical personalities who will run over you and steal your ideas to make them their own. They have an emptiness fulfilled by you because you were eager and looking for any handout of worthiness. They become selfish and controlling, as they know they can get by with it. Anger from someone scorned for these reasons can get very dangerous at this point because the "I will show you" syndrome infuses. It is similar to the "I won't get mad, but get even" reaction. This definitely is not a high-quality ingredient for healthy nacre.

If you can now view anger as a protective device then maybe it would be wise to understand what you are protecting. You are protecting your heart from fear in the end. Over the years, we innocently and naively open ourselves up to loving and trusting people. After many experiences of rejection to that love, we build up hard nacre of protective deflection. I believe the other phrase would be "the wall". We become cautious. Caution is ok, but learning the lessons and creating a love for who you are will attract the right person to you and the wall will not be necessary.

Life is refinement of finding your truth, not another's truth. What are you willing to give up to facilitate finding their truth? Some give up everything, become the martyr and resentment slowly unfolds to an unusual extent as fear and hurt slide by without a bit of notice. These people are usually caretakers and take a second seat to help the other. In the end, caretakers end up being disappointed and resentful while having taken no steps forward for their own growth and blame always goes to the other person. "Pity poor me for all I have done for them". One needs to take care of *Self* in order to take care of others. Depleted resources need monitoring to insure future resources are available when needed. Never taking responsibility for your shortcomings is dangerous. Never seeking the truth or making an honest attempt to overcome these possible bad habits will keep the dysfunction alive. Not all is lost. You always have the opportunity to begin with a new agenda and a new slate. You need to take honest stock in your own truths and decide if you are sick and tired of being sick and tired.

You may continue to expose unhealthy past reactions without realizing it, but each time you make a true effort to learn and not be afraid to dig deep into your own soul instead of dissecting the other, the reaction minimizes. Any expectation of an illusionary result creates anger. The more you can turn the illusion into truth, the better off everyone will be. Socrates said it best of all..."Know thyself and to thine own self be true". Remember?

⚜

Chapter 22
Denial

Denial can be so subtle you do not even perceive it as a form of rejection. Denial is simply not accepting the truth of an issue. Rejection is not being able to accept what may not be working in your favor. Lies do not work in your favor therefore rejection will most likely occur. All created by yourself. Perhaps truth is not always welcome because it can be scary information, which might cause us pain or heartache. So we live with the expectation life will change if we are patient or we delude ourselves into believing what is not certainty.

We tell ourselves one more day or one more detail to be clear about what I believe to be true, but that day gets pushed away for another week because the person you have dancing becomes a little wiser on keeping you deluded. We fool ourselves that all is calm for now and temporarily ignore the original illusion. We are now adding to the many untruths already in "the system" and so the layering begins. The explosion will come another day. We just need more data! We have a tendency to really build the bomb of data so when the explosion occurs it covers everything at once! Let us take out the whole city instead of a block at a time.

The specifics of truth always surface! Now and again, reality smacks you on the side of the head so hard you cannot possibly miss the point. On other occasions, it only makes your head twist to the side and you feel slightly puzzled by what you heard. It strikes a cord that just does not compute. It begins to fester and all of the other hidden and elusive data begin to surface until the pieces commence to joggle into place. Your intuition whispers to you, but you are not responding because the puzzle is still missing some pieces. We do not want to accuse people unjustly if we are unsure because it can damage trust a person has for another. It can be difficult to regain trust once broken. Now we become guarded. We keep one eye and one ear open until we feel comfortable again. So now the question remains to be answered "Is this an inherent part of their personality that will never change or is it behavior brought on because they were in a survival part of their life?" Need more data! This could go on for months or years. How long do you let it continue? How long do you have to go until you are sure what to do?

We know truth eludes us for many reasons. You would think we would become experts at identifying truths at some point. The obstacles to certainty could be due to our own insecurities, which resurface when something hits a nerve. We continue to sabotage our own happiness by reacting with old behavior. Jealousy does not feel good for anyone when it erupts. Do you continue to allow suspicion to consume you or are you willing to take a hard look at your own reality? If you can take the step to look deep inside yourself, take responsibility for your presentation of the data as you perceive it, you can communicate more effectively with the other person. They can choose to accept or deny your assessment. If you have value to them, they make the effort to understand and overcome any misinterpretation so everyone feels safe and secure. On the other hand, they could choose to exit because you are getting too close to their truth. They may feel your suspicion getting stronger and more accurate. It is a risk, but a risk that will give you the clarity you need to understand your validity truly exists.

An example of this could be someone in a relationship that has controlled everything about the partner to the point that the other person feels suffocated and enslaved. The enslaved person initially thought this person was strong and a take charge person. As time passed, the noose gets tighter. When the enslaved person begins to wake up to this revelation, the controlling person becomes even more controlling. They monitor phone calls, mail, chip away at the esteem of the enslaved person to weaken their retreat. This could escalate into physical abuse. The environment has been unsafe from the beginning, but the enslaved person was unaware and did not see any signs in the beginning because they actually needed someone to take control of their lives and allowed it to happen. Be careful what you wish for...it may come in abundance.

Identifying an exact pattern of false presentation can take some time. Subtle demeaning comments that can chip away at your esteem could be "the roots of your blonde hair have nothing to grow in", "You have no passion" or "Jim's wife looks good" with no compliment to you ever. How long do you allow yourself to continue searching for the answer? How it influences your standard daily living plays a key. The eruption of emotions can open the door to communicate your feelings, but the level of the flare-up can close the door as well. It is best to immediately identify and communicate to the other person the sensitivity involved before you lose the moment. If too much time passes, you probably will lose your nerve and truth defers again. Some people put up with your inability to communicate, as they may require your support in some way and the only way to keep your cooperation is to never let you hear the truth. They can also continue to get by with the secrets. They prefer you remain unclear. They may be insecure not having what you are providing and not want to rock the boat of provision. It is a never-ending cycle of dysfunction, which eventually erodes the esteem of the providing source for the demanding needs of the insecure. Never a good ending.

Rent the movie *Never-Ending Story*. It has hidden meanings, as many children's movies do, with reference to the darkness of negative thinking and living. I know there are those who would not consider watching a child's movie, but I have always noticed deep value in most children movies, which could benefit any age. I have been ridiculed a few times for watching "kid movies" at my age. This perception is unfortunate because I always will watch them. I will not allow someone to chip away at something I think has value. The movies are inspiring to me and leave me hopeful that children can still learn right from wrong or good from evil in the movies. Some parents have just fallen short of teaching this. Denial or fear of one's personal gifts and capabilities creates insecurity that burrows deep into the psyche. Usually someone has planted a misnomer in your psyche at some point that you have no gifts or abilities. We end up feeling we do not deserve the best in life and yet we say we want the best in life. We fall short of making it to the finish line and accept the first thing appearing to have promise. We also have a tendency to personalize derailing comments made by others that translate differently to us because we are already feeling weak and add yet another nail to the already embedded insecurities. A never ending story until you change the storylines.

There is nothing wrong with accepting less for a time as there may be a lesson needing improvement. My mother used to say there is no right or wrong to our decisions. You just make another decision. I wish she had understood her own words and I could have developed more quickly than I did. She had the tendency to want to make my decisions for me even after I was on my own. Until I became older and could articulate my decisions, right or wrong, it was a constant battle that took tough stubbornness in order to maintain my stand. Then she used to tell me I sound just like my father. I took that as a compliment, but I don't think it was meant that way. "You said there are no right or wrong decisions, so how can you say I am wrong? Let me experience my decision and I can know for myself." How can one argue with one's self? She backed off for the moment when I repeated her words back to her. I remember a scene in the show "Friends" that made me laugh and still does. Jennifer Aniston says to Joey while they are out sailing…"I was so busy trying not to be like my mother, that I became my father". A revelation, for sure, that we all experience at some point.

Reaching an enlightened crossroad like this can steer you back through an unaltered path of similar choices and end results or guide you into a brand new environment enhancing positive changes in your development. You need to ascertain what constitutes YOUR best path and have courage to follow it to completion. Acceptance of either path continues to refine or add to a healthier self-esteem. You will find vulnerabilities on either path, but both continue to compel you toward your truth. Truth is what we are striving

to achieve and each truth-uncovered allows new blossoms to emerge and the dead blossoms shrivel and
blow away. The old blossoms will fertilize new growth
for another person in need of a similar lesson.

Denial is the second step in the grieving process
following shock. Shock can last a short or long time
depending on how attached you were to your reality.
If someone dies or leaves you unexpectedly, you do not
usually have time to coach your thoughts. Your mind
tries to sort out matters unhandled between the two
of you and your motivation crashes for a time. The situation becomes surreal. You begin to question if you
could have done something to halt the exodus or prepare more effectively for emergencies. These obsessive pondering thoughts of possible difficulties could
essentially damage your spirit if your world was only
this person. Your abilities to love or prepare for your
future shut down. You are afraid that anyone you love
may leave unexpectedly, and convince yourself the
pain is not worth starting new. You convince yourself
to hold onto what was past out of loyalty to unfinished
business! You do not allow yourself to enjoy life and
you begin to wither from the inside out. You want
what can no longer be. I have found it takes about two
years to regain your equilibrium after a death or ending of a close relationship of someone who has been
very close to you. Some people jump right back in to
a relationship, like buying a new puppy to replace the

void, but is this truly best for you? Does it allow you time to reflect and process the importance of the loss, so maybe you can make changes in yourself? We all have the tendency to lose some of ourselves whether it is from loss of a close animal, a spouse or good friend who took up much of your alone time. We need the time in between to regain some of that back. Avoiding the pain and the process does not assist in your personal growth.

We generally are procrastinators and take much for granted when things become routine and comfortable. We do not usually take stock in developing ourselves until something shakes our tree. Then we may start grabbing for self help books, become depressed or use drugs and alcohol to numb any feeling. If you can get over the shock and denial in a short period, you may get angry with someone who left you in this position. Then again, maybe you are relieved it is all over and drop right into acceptance bypassing any depression. Much depends on your attachment and understanding of the reality you were living in and how much truth existed. If untruths surface, it may take longer to move into acceptance. You bounce back and forth trying to figure everything out because this reality was quite unfamiliar to you. First denials, then anger, back to denial, then depression, depression, depression and then anger and back to denial. You could remain in this whirlwind for quite some time until the truth settles into place. Sometimes the truth is not at your fingertips because people who could enlighten you will not talk. Anyone growing up in the depression era knows some conversations will never leak out because the shame attached is too great. Little did they know what was shameful then is commonplace now. Therefore, you could spend the rest of your life in the dark. If your opportunity for enlightenment about past family issues can never exist, and the information is buried with the keepers of the information, let go of the whole thing. It is no longer important to wonder. If it was meant for you to know, it will surface at some point. Get on with your life the way you want to live it. This is the goal anyway. Why clutter it up with details that have nothing directly to do with you anyway. It may provide an ah- ha for you, but you still need to deal with the present issues.

There comes a point in time when letting go of what you thought was real is necessary. If you could change others and their reality, you might be able to adjust the stage. Nevertheless, the hidden truths could eventually surface when you least expect it and when you most need it. So, enjoy life until that day comes. If changes need to occur because of this new data, deal with it at that time and have no regrets.

Chapter 23
Regrets of Life

Few people in the world have "no regrets" in their lifetime. My mother claimed to be one of them. She loved her work, her family and even her struggles apparently. I used to wonder how she could be satisfied because she appeared to live a very humble life. My brothers and I used to say she would be happy living in the basement on a cot. She had no hobbies and she participated little outside of work. She said when she was growing up; not much else existed. Her perception of life was apparently fulfilling to her even in the bad times of depression. There was no want of anything at her house other than what was in front of her. She had all she needed and her parents were able to provide many extras that most people did not have to keep any depressed times at bay. They managed to have fun as a family and welcomed visitors in to the house with food as the center of enjoyment. Many people were without consistent food sources and my grandparents enjoyed sharing this basic staple to maintain a pleasant bonding with friends who were not as fortunate. It was win-win for all. Card games were a way for them to change up the atmosphere. They appreciated the simple things in life.

My mother used to tell me I had to focus on a goal. I tried to explain there is so much out there, it is difficult to choose. Now in the age of transportation and computers, we realize introduction to the infinite world is available and finding our niche is not as cut and dried like "the old days". My mother said "back in the day", you were a nurse, secretary, teacher or homemaker. These were the only choices available. I believe she understood where I was coming from, but she still restricted what direction I was to follow employing her standards while under her roof. Venturing off into a field she was unfamiliar with created a lot of negative support that beat me down emotionally.

At 16, I wanted to be a food server or "waitress" back in the day. I was a kid wanting to make money, but my mother dismissed this option because she felt this was not respectable for a girl. I also wanted to work at the grocery store as a bagger like my brothers, but she said no. I did not understand why. I still do not, for that matter, except it was her reputation at stake instead of my learning to work and have money for myself. Therefore, I gave up. There was not much else for me to do in a small town. I became bored and lost passion for anything. She then called me "lazy". Talk about my confusion! I said, "you will not let me do anything, so what am I supposed to do? " She finally found me a job at the courthouse through a friend of hers. Apparently, this was acceptable to her reputation.

My point being, if she would have gotten out of her own way, I may have maintained some enthusiasm for my decisions. I would have eventually learned serving food or working at the grocery store was not for me, but it would have been my decision. There was no issue of life or death to my original desires, so let me fumble through my experiences. This is the unfortunate part of not having control of your life while under house rules. Therefore, yes, there are regrets in my past, but someone else limited my options and I had to oblige. I cannot change that past and I am not going to use my past as a "pity pot" to keep me from changing who I became to who I want to be. Somewhere in the myriad of lost direction, I not only mislaid my passions, but also had difficulty in finding my niche. I allowed others to find jobs for me because this was the pattern that I was familiar. It was easy and I was timid in interviews and did not like taking chances. I also felt less than because someone else was directing my decisions. This way of life became comfortable. I was comfortable being uncomfortable. Underneath all of this, I had a burning instinct to keep going and shed the skin so uncomfortable for me. As time passed, I realized I had control of my decisions and I slowly made changes. Those non-supportive opinions came from all directions to the point I had to move to the other side of the country to hear myself think and to begin a life that was mine.

Exposure to a certain lifestyle in your formative years leads you right into the same lifestyle pattern until you recognize the problem and make the decision to change. Most of the time you cannot even realize you are going there until you are there again. The down side for me was losing direction and finding jobs that did not fit my capabilities or desires and my self esteem started to hit bottom. By this time, I did not know what desires or capabilities I had to offer. I just knew what I was doing was not for me. I wondered if I would ever find passion for anyone or anything again. I felt dead inside.

How I wished for an answer. I went through many years with hit and miss jobs. I never really had a career in my mind. I had visions, but the visions fell short of the final goal. The closest I came was becoming self-employed as a consultant re-organizing companies. The only reason I "fell" into this field was my ex-husband was not reaching any goals with "our business" and I finally said, "let me go with you on your next call". We sold the next client. This could have been coincidence or luck and as we discussed, who cares as long as it happened. From that point on, I was the main partner in development of that business and successful. I still did not feel the passion, but I began to feel more confident again. I knew I was getting close, but was still a long way from where I needed to be. I maintained this status until I made major changes in my life, which included divorce, and moving to a brand new city knowing no one. This was actually a need. My first year or two was spent pulling myself off the ground due to sheer exhaustion of trying to live others' ideal of what and who I should be. I always put 150% of me into what ever I did whether it was a relationship or work. I began to wonder why I always ended in exhaustion. I took care of others and left nothing for myself. I was looking so far out for my enthusiasm and passion I failed to look where it resided: In my own heart and self.

I started back on the same path of finding "jobs" because I was exhausted from the consulting and marriage and I knew no other way. I did not care what, but wanted to try something new. Again, I "fell" into the restaurant business through a friend and said "why not?" This was something I wanted to try when I was young and did not get to experience because my mother had control. Well, now I am feeling in control of my life and my decisions for once, so I accepted the position. I did not care what it paid and I have nobody to tell me "NO". I actually remember feeling "rebellious" by accepting this position and I was determined to make up for those lost desires.

Who knows, I might like it. I realized, at this point, I might be on a detoured path for a while to make those decisions I could not make before. Whether it was out of spite or just to experience life did not matter at this point. It was my decision. I was with the restaurant for 5 years and again became exhausted, as it was an all day-night deal. It was a wonderful experience for me, but alas, not my passion.

The jobs I found always seemed to follow a path of people taking advantage of my skills and workaholic tendencies (as this is what happened to her), so exhaustion always seemed to follow me. I allowed this because I had no esteem yet. My mother took care of this when I was younger. I did meet some wonderful people and the "jobs" served a purpose in my new life. I realized, on my own, I did not desire to jump around forever. Maybe I could have saved myself 5 years, if my Mom had let me try it when I was sixteen. I now faced the new dilemma of finding another paycheck. I was finished with the restaurant business. I liked it, but it was not my passion.

Boy, what a pattern I maintained. Another friend offered a position at a psychiatric hospital. I always thought working in a hospital would be cool, so I accepted. That was 12 years ago and presently as I write this book, I am still there. I still never considered it a career, but a job. Until I find my enthusiasm,

I chose to stop looking for my passion. I honestly did not think either existed anymore. Whatever my Mom did buried all connections to my natural gifts. The one thought that reassured me was I knew I would be good at whatever the passion turned out to be because I always excelled in whatever I did. I felt like the jack-of-all-trades and master of none.

I cannot say I figured things completely on my own, but with the help of some spiritual mentors, I began to start visualizing possibilities for my passion. I reviewed what I liked and disliked and what I naturally excelled in from my experiences. Doubt crept in repeatedly and my mother's words kept numbing any immediate enthusiasms I tried to ignite. I would hash and rehash the desired possibilities until I hashed it to death. I would leave it alone for a while and, in time, pieces of intuition would start to filter back through to my mind's eye. They were pieces I needed to start seeing a new picture. I had to isolate from others to allow any of this to appear because others have this great need to throw in their "input" which I was tired of receiving.

I would wear the new vision for a while to see how it affected my enthusiasm. In all honesty, I am not at full passion yet as I write this book. What I know for fact is my capability to write, speak in public and find solutions for everyone else's issues. No matter where I am, this is easy and has always been a constant in my life. I still have the doubting audience made up of friends and family who ask me what credentials I think I have that I can write a book on self-help and speak about it. I stopped trying to justify myself to them and continued to pursue my goals without blessings from anyone. I do not talk about my future with anyone. If I do talk about my goals and there is any sign of negative incantation, I clam up again. I figure the proof will be in the results of my efforts. If I do not succeed, at least I continue moving in a direction that keeps me productively busy for quite awhile. This direction hopefully will create or dig up the passion I lost many years ago. Achieving that passion is the most important thing for me and the journey to get there may include leaving others behind or out of my life completely. I do not have the tolerance or patience for any person to slow me down at this point in life. Been there, done that already and life is too short.

I would imagine my third book will have the final answers to my personal quest and if things go as I foresee, I will have restored my passion. I have been without it for so long, I almost fear how my body will react to having positive current running through it all the time. The one subject matter I never gave up on was my "self". I have always had an underlying drive forward to find answers and the stamina for being stubborn until I got answers. That was a gift from both parents. I rarely allowed others to have control over my decisions for long. I might take that detour just to see where it went, but as I grew older, I was able to move off the non-productive path before more time was wasted. As you get older, you realize you have little time to waste and your intuition needs to be your best friend.

I read books; I observed people and assessed people who said, "I love what I do". I asked questions, I pondered, I cradled others to inspire their directions and if they understood what I was saying and truly desired change, they made it happen! I even got to the point where I said to myself "Why am I able to make it happen for others and not myself?" Of course, as you can read, it takes awhile for me to comprehend my own words.

They say people teach what they need to learn. I chewed on this concept for a long time. It is true. Over time, through experiences, more data and interaction with others, you will inadvertently put all the pieces together when you least expect it. Your own words begin to make sense. You will have an epiphany of truth or an "ah ha". You will say to yourself this makes sense now. Your body will shiver and your mind will not be able to release the newly formulated vision fast enough. That is excitement!

The outcome of telling my tales is to reinforce it may take years and many detours to find your way to peace and contentment. If you are like me, the goal is to keep moving forward. Do not become stuck and complain someone else is the problem or past limitations keep you from your passion. The only regrets a person should have are to stop trying altogether. You can only do what you can do and to stop your journey will only actuate the beginning of the end. We are here to learn, to overcome and grow as a person. Maybe the detours are what you needed to find your way. Most of us had parents who stifled our growth and imagination in someway or created self-limitation out of fear. They also gave us gifts, on the other hand, that bequeath us strength to uncover what they buried. My mom and dad taught me honesty, integrity, follow through, stubborn determination and provided the security and stability we needed as a family to keep going in the face of embarrassments and life changing events. There is always some dysfunction to deal with, but that dysfunction can be the irritation that begins your pearl development. People will believe what they want despite what you say. So why allow their doubts to keep you limited. My regret would have been allowing others to continue blocking my journey. The key is trust in yourself and know what is right for you will come if you continue to seek it out.

Chapter 24
Fun and Laughter

Some people become so rigidly conditioned at a young age to "grow up", they do not even recollect how to have fun as every year passes. They suppress their youthful side because others may have a disparate opinion of keeping the *Peter Pan syndrome* alive. We allow their judgment to influence our lives. One stops being a child because someone said to stop. Of course, too much of anything is not good. You do not want to be a Peter Pan completely either. You want to mature by being respectful of age and parallel the boundaries and responsibilities. We talked about this in the last chapter of regrets. How often does one talk them selves out of "fun" because you hear a tape in your head that says you are too old? Where do you draw the line?

A scenario relayed to me in an educational seminar made sense regarding an obsessive motivation "to have". Visualize yourself in a swimming pool chasing a most wanted beach ball. It always manages to stay out of reach the more you chase it. When you stop, the ball eventually returns to you. Life has similar lessons to offer when you intensely focus on results and you do not stop and smell the roses. Do all you can to achieve results daily and then take time to balance yourself by having relaxation time. If you continue to push yourself to the end with no reserves, you may not be able to enjoy the finish line, let alone get there. The beach ball will catch up to you. That is a promise. If you plant the seeds and water the plants, growth will eventually peek out from the depths of the darkness. You need to keep tending the soil to insure the environment is conducive for growth possibilities. Tending the soil could be eating good food, sleeping well and minimizing abuse to your body, soul and spirit.

Knowing when to take a break requires understanding your self. When your mind blocks, you become frustrated, errors begin to occur, agitation sets in, and your fists clinch. It is probably time to take a break. Do not ignore these signs. If unattended, physical vulnerabilities may take over. As I have mentioned before, I personally need to take "alone time" from people in general because I have a tendency to absorb outside energy that is not my energy and it strains my body. The stresses of other people can and will affect you and add to your own created stress. Did you ever feel like getting away from someone because negativity and problems hovered around them? It is draining!

The people who will not allow themselves to be alone never feel refreshed. Many hate being alone at any age or simply do not know how to be alone. They will stay in a bad situation or with someone longer than they should because of the trepidation of being alone. They keep people around all the time. To maintain the collegiate status of "life of the party", folks collect acquaintances to boast an arsenal of diversions in case boredom creeps into the picture. One needs an arsenal because the majority of people have busy lives and families, so the more calls one can make, *the numbers game*, the better chances someone will have time to play when needed. The quality of life is skewed somewhat by diversion.

What happened to quality of life? Are having 300 friends on face book, texting and twittering more important than existing quietly within your own world? Have you taken the time to notice your world has fallen apart and you are alone because obsession of living in everyone else's world through a non—interactive box has taken control?

What does quality of life mean to you? I would venture to guess most people do not take the time to anticipate the requirements for this. Each requirement is, of course, unique to each person and the norm is to fall into a decent quality of life when we are too old to enjoy it for long. It seems too risky to attempt it at an age when peer pressures keep us on the road of "keeping up with the Joneses". I admit, technology is fun and makes life exponentially expanded. We are reaching out to the externals for all our enthusiasms, so when taken away, we do not know what to do with ourselves. What happened to conversation?

I went to a ranch in California known for no TVs, radios, telephones or Internet hookup. The first time I went I did not know what to do with myself once my bags were unpacked. There were no stores for shopping and not much life within a few miles of the compound. My mind wandered a bit anxiously on what to do with myself. The first thought was a bath, which I reminisced I had not done in ages. There was no one to answer to or keep me from it and I did not have to worry about the phone ringing. I thought that sounded very nice! There is nothing like the re-alization you had not done something so simple be-cause of diversions. I then took a walk of the grounds (because I had time with no distraction) and became acquainted with the beauty of this oasis in the desert.

By now, I was relaxed and felt hungry. I believe it was only 5:00 pm at this time and my thought was how long could I stretch dinner out? I actually had more than 30 minutes to enjoy my meal. (Work al-lots me 30 minutes) After dinner, I went back to the casita and lay on the bed to read. It was 6:30 pm and I realized I was tired so I thought a nap seemed appropriate and why not? I slept through the whole night. Again, I realized no one was going to call or ring the doorbell to disturb me in any way. I never felt so delightful in my life! The next day, I walked around the compound looking at flowers, animals, and reading about hot springs. God forbid, the next thing I did was pick up a book! After reading some, I started taking pictures of even the smallest of things I would never have noticed otherwise. I was having fun with myself!

The point is I began to find things to do. If there had been a cell phone or computer, (which had no service there) I probably would have been on one of them or someone would have been calling me. I forced myself to look at what I was missing and now I ogle when I see others obsessed with their cell phones. Look up and see what else is around. Try to have a day with no cell phone or computer. Leave them at home. Experience the change to your mind's capabilities and directions. It is an unbelievable instantaneous result and if you can accept the choice to take a complete break from the world and follow through with it, the value is worth more than money can buy.

We only allow ourselves a small portion of time to experience quality of life if we even grasp a portion at all. When we get to a certain age, we begin to let go of things that no longer have importance to us. We get tired of hanging on to what the Jones' expect of us. Excuses surface about time constraints, lack of money, need for money, you do not like being around someone or there is no one to accompany you. Some of this may be true and some may be reasons to politely exit a situation you are not interested. For example, if you are in a long-term relationship, maybe you continue to watch movies that waste your time because your companion insists you watch. Do you make trade offs or find something that is more fulfilling to you?

What else can these excuses mean? If fun is a stranger to you, it may be an avoidance of your own reality or fear of losing control and crossing boundaries others believe you should not partake. The more you deny yourself healthy pleasure, understand your truth has probably morphed into something you do not recognize. Your enthusiasm for innocent play has been stepped on, abused, numbed, and just plain lost. Passion for life has left the building. Maintaining or understanding your passion has to include fun and laughter.

People tend to feel "fun" means juvenile conduct and yet we admire those people who seem to maintain enthusiasm for the juvenile activities. At the hospital, we had patients, in the beginning of admission, actually resist art and craft groups because they were too depressed or so spent they had no energy. Some said they did not come here to have fun. I rest my case. When encouraged to attend as a therapeutic process, they finally relented and thereafter look forward to the group. Social skills increased, energies increased and they became close to the other people involved in the groups. They have nothing to lose in that environment because it is safe to have fun. Who is going to point the finger when everyone is participating?

The hospital includes this as a large part of therapy and we certainly still care what others expect do we not? What else do you have to do anyway since incarceration temporarily limits your options to work and communicate with the outside world? Your mind starts to justify time spent. No one has to see me. This is all confidential. One may as well go to this group because there is nothing else to do. In time, it develops into a similar venue as the compound I attended. As it were, I took my own self time out by going to the ranch. The result is the same in the end. Sometimes we are forced to nourish our souls and sometimes we follow our instincts and do it on our own. Some may get massages or take a vacation. Others may read a book or take a ride in a car. Make the time to refresh your soul with no distraction.

Digging deep into the dysfunctional psyche is draining! There is much clutter not understood or even known. You need to allow your brain rest through this process and play with rest allows this. You can do it on your own or with a group. Peers with similar situations can ultimately be one of your best therapists and playtime is a non-threatening form of interaction. They may have processed a similar issue before your arrival and now became the educator with an appropriate outlook that makes sense to you. Peers can be your best cheerleaders! The group begins to bond because everyone is taking the time to understand and empathize with each other! This could occur in social settings as well. It does not have to be a structured process.

People in general, like helping others overcome obstacles. Everyone finds it easier to help someone else in need than help themselves anyway. Discerning their input will be your obstacle turned skill. Do they have your best interests at heart or are they so un-enlightened they harbor envy or selfishness for your goals? Strangers may be the rescuer and help you grasp issues never considered and a stranger can be blatantly honest. What do they have to lose? They barely know you, so there is no fear of rejection or abandonment! I have had strangers be more helpful to me than my close friends and family. Sometimes, the closer you are to someone the more difficult it is to learn from them. You begin to filter words and thoughts for fear of rejection or not communicate at all for fear of the same.

Why is it so difficult to be non-judgmental in our personal and intimate relationship issues? In one word, it is "fear". We are so quick to judge others with or without the facts because we learned to do this. People feel more powerful when they have all the answers. Fear of not having control of the self diverts all attention to the other person. Verbalizing other people's foibles justifies enough diversion from our life problems and rationalizes minimal review of our own life. Judging others usually ends in fights or misunderstandings because it hurts to feel someone is not listening to you. One wonders how a person can say these atrocities and judge without knowing the facts. Perception and reality can clearly be two different things. Pay attention to people throwing their judgment into your situation with no care or thought of knowing all the facts of your situation or where you reside on your life path. The more stress one feels, the more fear takes hold.

Fun and laughter can cause fear to take a back seat. Bob Hope provided shows utilizing this very concept for our military. The troops were able to relax for a while and enter the unknown of war with less fear and anguish. Their souls regenerated. They bonded to their purpose and each other with branded memories of shared laughter that carried them through some very stressful times. Bob Hope could very well have won the war for America in an indirect but powerful way!

Fun does not have to be expensive. You do not need to play costly games such as golf, tennis, or anything physically inclined if you are not able, but you can involve yourself in pottery, photography or even card games if that is your preference. Read books which interest you. Write poetry or a fiction novel of your life. We know "truth is better than fiction". The names were changes to protect the innocent. Computers are making loners out of people, but if being a loner is where you want to be then use it to do something creative for yourself. I know a person, who attends yard sales buying whatever and then sells on eBay. She found something she enjoys and ultimately creates some interaction as well as gets her out of the house. She not only makes some money, but she does not become stagnant. There is still little direct interaction with people, but she enjoys this as her needed stimuli.

My roommate hosts a youth sports festival presently in San Diego and Minnesota, which introduces children under the age of 13 to sports and music. He hopes to expand it nationally. The festival's main directive is to fight childhood obesity and attempts to persuade children into team activities rather than sitting at home eating or playing on the computer all the time. He has a mentoring group from every venue of sport to demonstrate their specific skill to a child that may never have had the opportunity to play. They can be involved or not, but it will be a safe environment for them to learn. To introduce any sport or activity to a child may excite them into sustainable movement that could change the direction of their lives. It promotes healthy eating and enables the whole family to participate. It creates a bonding, which humans need. No man is an island in the end. We need others to share in the good and the bad. Watching children run from one event to the next can be fun because for them each one is new and exciting. Children are a nice reminder that uncluttered minds revel in excitement and fun. As a parent, you chose to have the child, so do all you can to nurture what excites your child. I do not think God eliminated fun from adult lives. The older we get and the more dysfunction we hold onto, the more clutter builds up like plaque and inhibits the free flow of enthusiasm. I always wonder what direction I would have taken sooner if my parents had understood the importance of nurturing my enthusiasm instead of suffocating it.

I love to watch some of the old comedians like Johnny Carson, Dean Martin or George Goble. As mentioned earlier, Bob Hope was a saint to our military because he could make people laugh. I remember an announcer said one of the Bob Hope shows took place prior to boys actually going into battle the next day and he couldn't believe how they were able to laugh a few hours before the possibility of getting killed. Camaraderie, trust and a common bond can develop through laughter alone. We also know the health benefits of laughter are beneficial at any age. You are calmer, stress minimizes and problems disappear even for a short time. You develop trust in knowing miracles can happen and the end justifies the means. We are a country that enjoys freedom and even anticipation of death becomes a conviction to fight for all who believe in the same ideal.

Laughter can increase productivity at home, work and the classroom. You want to get up in the morning. You may consider someone more effective when they can laugh at reality. Reality can be funnier than made up scripts. Look how people love the blooper type shows or funniest home videos of everyday life.

So you see, laughter and fun do exist with value and watching innocent children laugh at the smallest of details can warm your heart and bring a smile to your face. You do not want to lose that innocent adventurous child in you. Your ego may keep you from watching a cartoon, drawing in a coloring book or experience riding a carousel. How many times do you watch an activity and wish you could play but you stop because others think you are not acting your age? Who wants to get old? We spend millions of dollars to look young. You need to feel young to maintain it. You are creating old age by deafening your inner child and stifling your experiences to try anything sensible, but fun. Fun eludes you because it does not fit into society's age developmental mold. Of course, I am not suggesting inappropriate behavior that could hurt or embarrass another. That is not fun or funny.

Set aside some time each day to enjoy even 10 minutes in nature. Surround yourself with color; listen to music, which engenders a feeling of movement or calmness depending on your mood. Turn the cell phone and computer off! You will begin to feel inspired and refreshed exponentially. The creative thoughts commence to flow automatically.

I love having color around me! People tend to use browns, blacks and neutrals because there is less exertion to keep clean and non-stimulating for the children. Instead of the world adjusting to us, we adjust to the world. Neutral colors can be calming, but try to balance those shades with some vibrant pictures or flowers to offset coming to a complete stop when you arrive home. Your home is your castle, so make it say and do what you want to feel. Balance. Not everyone's taste will correspond, but compromise of a small area may be all you need to keep you inspired.

The senses of visual, sound, touch, taste, and imagination allows children the joy of life, which continually stimulates their vision and surpasses "the boring box" we inhabit as adults. Why do you think Disney is so successful? Fantasy at all ages is stimulating! The biggest error we make is to dismiss any enthusiastic thought and cram it back into the psyche to lay dormant and rot. The cycle of self-disparagement will increase until we have crippled our self mentally and physically. Find something that ignites your senses! You do not need to be a child to experience what God offers in variety for any age. Movies can fulfill this time if you cannot leave or no money is readily available. Again, I will reiterate reading a book as a lost art. Combine action with your inherent desires and capabilities. Who knows, you may find your passion.

Chapter 25
Having a Plan!

My roommate actually suggested this as a chapter topic and I feel it agreeably follows the sequence of ideas discussed already. I believe we have chatted about the absolute necessity for taking action to accomplish goals. You cannot sit home and dream without taking steps toward the dream. You have to begin somewhere to make the dream a truth. You can read every self-help book available on a subject, but if you do not put the information into practice, it is useless to your growth. You become the person who teaches and still yet needs to learn that which you teach.

The first step is a big one! The ideal is to know where you want to go and map out the roads before you begin. Of course, this is having a plan! Most use a map when traveling to insure a smooth journey from point A to B. There are fewer complications and you can plan your fun time when things become temporarily stagnant. You always have the choice to make changes and adjustments to modify the path and actually, this would be normal. Rarely does anything run the exact way you plan.

I cannot think of many goals in my past that followed the precise plan I originally set forth. Actually, to date, there are none. The problem I incurred was planning my life goals around what others felt I should be doing. At times, I hit one wall briefly. Other times, I diverted off my track so much I hit multiple walls sequentially, but always seemed to attain a new experience from something I never would have experienced otherwise and usually without consequence to me. I never had a regret for hitting that wall.

I knew I had to be "blessed" because I was close to some lives that were obviously the wrong direction for me and I came through it unscathed as I said earlier. The only thing I lost was time. I hit more walls than anyone, but I kept trudging through all those unsolicited opinions of what I should do with myself. I guess that is where my stubbornness came in handy. So I figured until my main show begins again, it was like an educational commercial, walking beside the life of others and not really being a part of the picture.

Of course, walls exist because the universe is telling you it is not the direction to take or at least not at the moment. Sometimes the walls I hit were clear because I would take a good look what was on the other side. Other times, the walls were opaque. I actually came to understand a wall means, "Wrong way- do not enter" whether it is clear or opaque. This perception was formulated from years of slamming into walls. Instead of dreading the wall, I would process a way around it and in time, I became faster in moving around the wall and more comfortable with the decision to do this. The distinction is I kept moving even though I had no clue what door was going to finally open and allow me to continue on my path.

I believe this is how one differentiates between jobs and careers. You interview for a job and your skills do not always meet the job requirements. A job provides a paycheck though and some rarely plan more than getting a paycheck. A few wait for a raise or a promotion and there is no real design to change unless it is into another job that has nothing to do with the last. A career can provide fulfillment of a talent that expands a desired path for growth by a craving to enhance a specialty. There can be a natural progression toward a goal based on experience. You would assume a career would have fewer obstacles and maybe this is true if you chose the right career. Perhaps the career you chose has outlived its purpose and your personal need is to take another path. All of this is normal.

Change is normal. What is not normal is stopping movement altogether. You begin to sing the "what if I...". You become immovable. Negative thoughts begin to make a person cynical of anyone who has "more" and envy starts to eat away at you. Now is a good time to take that fun break, look at what your life has become, and see what you want to make it. Eliminate the doubts, listen to your intuition and take the first step to plan. You cannot pour over where others may be because you compare yourself to a situation not the same. They may have their own issues you cannot see even with all of the "toys" to occupy them. Remember, "All that glitters is not always gold".

When things become confusing or frustrating; stand still, have some fun and let the beach ball make it back to you when the chase meets a temporary reprise. Enjoy those moments of being idle! A door always opens at some point if you are being diligent and focused on the steps of the plan. Follow every lead that comes your way whether it sounds weird or unusual. I have found your pearl lies where you least expect it. It hides behind another door or rock. If you stop moving and working the plan, you may miss the connection.

Did you ever turn down a situation you did not want to initially attend? Someone invites you out and you resist going, but eventually you give in to the opportunity. It turns out to be the best thing that ever happened to you! Either you meet someone who you personally connect with or they associate with someone you need. An idea may even come to you because you are distracted from the normal stress of making it happen. A nice leisure activity enables your mind to rest and intuition pops through. Your puzzle begins to take form again and commences to revive the visual picture you painted in your mind way back at point A and maybe now with a few changes.

Of course, if you are lucky to have time and money, planning a direction that suits your fancy can be easy to a point. It still requires planning! Taking any risk is the hurdle and having a support system certainly helps. However, poor planning and management of the risk will get you in trouble every time. Risk is a gamble, but if your enthusiasm comes from your heart, the direction feels right, you prepare and manage your plan with integrity, the doors will open.

You may not have any support system and have to count on your drive alone to lead you through the forest of "what ifs". There is always choice and having an attitude of faith in yourself will overcome any doubters that follow in hot pursuit of your failures. You know it is a choice you want for yourself and a thick skin is necessary to realize failure may only be a temporary wall identifying another option to achieve the same goals. Once you start, be open to what comes your way on the journey. Consistent movement is the necessary key to make anything happen. ❦

Chapter 26
Your Passion for Life

Your passion comes from your heart. It is a strong and compelling emotion like being in love. You know it is true and correct and your excitement brings life to all who expose themselves to your passion. Passion can be addictive and infectious, just as laughter is contagious. The world has a passion for freedom and peace while on earth. It is a desire from the heart. However, like our lives, passion can be lost because of universal greed and needs. The world loses sight of the whole picture because they can only see their own back yard. Computers and media are bringing these worlds closer together and people are seeing things they may be missing and desire. Some crave it all for themselves. The fast pace and constantly changing world of technology has put most everyone in a high-speed lane and patience has become outdated. We do not take time to look at ourselves for fear of missing progress, so why should we take time to understand anyone else? At some point, we will spin out from exhaustion unless we find our own grounding source that keeps us balanced. It does not exist externally.

We talked about the balance of good and evil, love and hate, and day and night. There are those who have the same obsession for evil to prevail. We would never understand how someone could have this type of "passion", but when it is not for the good of all, is it really passion or selfish desire? Selfish desire does not come from the heart, but from the head. It comes from neediness and a desire to control. Opposites exist for us to know the effects of each and the different outcomes both offer. Many fairy tales exist for children to understand evil never wins in the end if our true passion exists for the better part of all. The only thing evil provides is miserable emptiness, darkness, and depression. Malevolence suffocates real passion.

Evil can take on so many roles in our lives. It can mask itself as a parent who takes no role in raising a child to know right from wrong. It can be a person who wants to rule the world or just the department of your company. Words alone can destroy someone's passion by belittling or bullying. Evil can be drugs and alcohol used to the point of dysfunctional living. A person cannot hold a job, your family leaves you, or no one wants to be around you because you have learned to manipulate them with lies. Youth requires encouragement of self-esteem so they can cope with the evils of adulthood. They become unmotivated and a barnacle sucking the life out of someone because they do not have anything and do not want to work for it. The biggest destruction of passion for me is not allowing a child to dream and be involved in the fantasy of creation normal to every child. I still have wonderful anticipation of Christmas, Easter and the Tooth fairy! I may not celebrate Easter quite the same as when I was a child, but I still love the thrill of what it represents. Then again, why not create an atmosphere in your house for the holiday or season you loved? Take and make the time to color some eggs if nothing more.

I remember my first year of marriage; we were not going to put up a Christmas tree. We were planning to go to the parents' home so we figured there was no point. Three days before Christmas, we changed our minds. We bought and decorated a fresh tree, and it was amazing how we felt more festive! We get lazy and assume there is no point to decorate or bake if no one is going to be around. Do it for yourself. Be grateful you can still feel the get-up-and-go to create. Keep change as an active part of your life. People who are not flexible to change will stagnate. Change is inevitable and necessary. When you get into the routine, mundane motion, which plants you in front of a TV or computer every day, stop yourself. Shake up your routine. Plan for it. Every Monday, Wednesday and Friday, I will attend the gym. Every Tuesday, Thursday and Saturday, I will walk along the beach. At any time, you can change your plan if it does not work or becomes boring. That is the glory of being human. We can make another decision! You can render change to your routine.

Throughout all this movement, you are looking for something that inspires you and you alone. You are not tagging along on someone else's' passion. Of course, it is nice to be a part of their passion, but you begin to lose some of yourself if you do not nourish your own spirit. There is room in the house for two people to have two different passions. Maybe they can go hand in hand. You can participate in theirs when you are feeling temporarily blocked and vice versa. The enthusiasm created will help keep the passion in the relationship or the family. You will be a role model by setting the example.

Children naturally mimic parental behavior and if they see you sitting, they will sit. If they see you are an active person, they will follow suit if this behavior is encouraged. We already know children may resist in the beginning, but think back to the chapter where we discussed encouragement of new adventures. This helps develop their self-esteem. The more they experience, the more they can relate and make decisions about what they like or dislike in life. Sheltering children "from the world" is no way to help them learn to cope with the world.

What does this have to do with finding your passion? It seems simple to me. The more you experience in life, the more you know about your personal likes and dislikes as well as what you are naturally good at doing and what you are not good at doing. These facets will steer you back to a probable past intuitive flash, which has occurred at many points already in your life, and you doubted it away. I have ignored those intuitive flashes many times and it kept resurfacing over the years until I did not have a choice but to see it, feel it and know my intuition was getting more intense for me to pay attention. I always felt there had to be something more for me because I have no children and I was very good at everything it seemed, but master of none. I just did not seem to have a passion for anything. Even though discontent followed me for many years, I never gave up trying to figure it out.

I reviewed my past to date and pulled out all things I excelled in, what I liked and what I felt I was supposed to do. I had help from spiritual counselors; meditations, books and anything I could come across that would help me uncover my passion. I never gave up on new experiences and knowledge, but I had to keep most thoughts to myself because there are too many people who will try to plant doubt in the mind. Those people are usually the ones closest to you, so beware! Hold your passion close to your heart and seek out those who will share your passion. Do not give up if you feel it is for the good of all and most especially for you. Leave the others to their miseries.

Chapter 27
Finding Your Heart

The contentment felt in your heart is the single most important part of your peace. I am not speaking so much in a physical sense but in the end, lack of contentment may become or already is a physical complication. Your thoughts become your future. Does your heart ache? Are you having heart problems? Are you afraid to experience life and therefore have no life? Are you always financially broke and therefore visualize poverty forever? Are you afraid to love and therefore have no one to love? Do you see how there is a correlating parallel?

The heart takes a beating in this life. We tend to protect the heart by transferring the pain into work, drugs, loneliness or depression to name a few. We create unhealthy nacre of our heart and soul by dismissing our own needs of love and acceptance. We learn ways to avoid the effort it takes to look inside ourselves. We have gone through periods of giving up ourselves to please others. We convince ourselves that being alone or numbing our feelings of pain is the only way to salvage what is left of our self. We find an escape from the anguish, but it continues to follow us. We lose the energy of enthusiasm because we keep waiting for someone to save us. Where does it end?

Sometimes we feel outside circumstances force us to accept where we are and not where we want to be. Fear keeps us stuck. Everyone needs to become responsible for their own happiness. In the end, if you make an honest effort to make needed changes, you will begin to break free of many acquired fears, which would continue to manifest those doubts and old tapes of being less than what you can become if you don't make any effort. Your heart will sing again and love for all will begin to re-enter the picture. Motivation comes from a heart that feels free. If your heart is blocked off, no one is going to motivate anyone unless they choose to be motivated. If it does not feel right for you, it probably is not right for you.

When you start making positive changes for yourself, false parts of yourself and pseudo friends fall away. Know that you are building a new foundation that works for you. Change is going to be awkward and can be a lonely road for a while until you meet up with those who understand and support your new authentic self. The only protection you will need is your ability to feel judgment coming your way, deflecting these judgments with confidence in the words you speak, and the actions you continue to exhibit. Your path will be unaffected. Your pearl is beginning to shine!

Release yourself from toxic people, food and environments and you will find your cravings for those toxic resolutions change into cravings for healthy resolutions. You will feel more kindly to others and insecurity will melt away. Your heart pumps better, you sleep better, you handle problems more easily and you feel comfortable communicating what you truly feel without fear of rejection. If someone does not like what you have to say, they can move on and you are the better for letting them go.

It would be unnatural to never need reassurance now and again. It would also be unnatural to assume you do not need others to help you along the way. Again, my mother engrained in us never to let anyone see or know if there is a problem which basically meant to me we never ask for help. If there is a problem, we will handle it on our own. There were so many times I followed this conditioning until I realized I did not have all the answers to my problems. I grew up in a small town that provided minimal stimulation and diversification and then add the restrictions my parents placed on me, it is amazing I ever made it out of there to seek the answers I needed to grow.

One of my high school teachers apparently saw something special for me. I never believed my parents would agree, but God bless her for giving me an opportunity to get out of my prison. The teacher was acquainted with someone in Europe and arranged for me to school in Belgium. My parents miraculously agreed and the rest is history. The first three weeks were difficult because I was in a strange place with new people and a language I did not know. I adapted quickly and realized this was an opportunity to see more than I ever dreamed about and I never looked back ever again. I felt saved. My curiosity and enthusiasm began to resurface. I still had many hot coals to walk on to overcome my instilled fears, but this was a new beginning for me. That teacher must have sensed something even more than I did and I will never forget. I had become numb, as many do, blocked at every new turn, desires bashed and all opportunities remained out of reach or passed by before I knew they existed. There always seemed to be a reason to accept nothing from the universe. If you did not do it by yourself, it must not be valid. This was according to the gospel of Ruth, my mother.

Attempting any unplanned or untried ventures, following through with my aspirations and tuning out my mother were the most difficult obstacles for me to overcome. You want to tell your mother and father the good and bad experiences, but when you meet with objection and negativity every time, no matter whether good or bad, you find you minimize what you tell them. My father was actually good about listening without judgment and therefore he earned as much information about me as I knew he could handle.

Parents can also sabotage your freedom and happiness by quietly putting wedges in between you and your desire. When exposed or confronted, they manage to persuade you there was no malicious intent on their part. They are our parents and they would NEVER get in the way of our happiness! The parent may actually have a fear of losing you or control of you. They keep you dependent on them emotionally or financially so they can control you with guilt or money. If you do not oblige their true dependence on you, your feelings of disloyalty to that parent stifles your continued growth. These are the worst chains of all. They keep you prisoner from your own life. I had someone tell me their mother would disown them if they married and to date they are still not married. This same woman turned away the love of her life. She now has such bitterness toward her 95-year-old mother because at her age of 65 she still takes care of the mother. She remains an unmarried resentful caretaker. Her mother continues to live with her holding her in chains from which she is too weak to escape.

My grandmother locked my Dad in his room at 21 so he would not see my mother prior to their marriage. He broke down the door and never returned to live in that house. My grandmother as much admitted she raised him for her purposes and she was not going to share him with anyone. It did not matter if it was my mother or another female, she was going to do everything in her power to poison the situation and stand back cleaning her hands of deceit. My father, out of loyalty, maintained a mother/son relationship, but on his terms and he never allowed her to interfere with his marriage or raising his children. My grandmother continued to try and poison the relationship in subtle ways and even tried to poison my own relationship with my mother. My mother had her faults but she was always honest and giving and I knew the truth. The poisoned attempts met with failure at every turn.

Parents have their own needs and insecurities and identifying their problems makes them imperfect. We expect and want our parents to be perfect, but alas, everyone has a cross to bare. They have issues to overcome as well. If you take a stand to be free of their constraining imperfections they drop into your lap, you will blossom. Their baggage is their baggage, not yours. They may never change their ways. Accept who they are and realize their problems are not your problem unless you allow fear of rejection or abandonment to win. If you truly feel they will abandon you because you do not respond the way they want you to, their hold on you can be exasperating. They should want you to be happy. If their heart is hurting, they should not be superimposing their hurt onto you so you innately follow the same path. Everyone wants the respect of their parents and parents use this to control your decisions if they have selfish motives.

Any relationship between two people can have the same results if selfishness exists in just one person. The other person tries so hard to overcome the selfish person's pain only to realize they are fighting the battle alone. Selfishness continues to seek out the givers of the world and when the giving stops due to someone's reality check, it would be a rare person who recognizes they are doing something wrong and change to balance the scales of what is right. Change is not easy. It can happen, but what is the value to you in the end? How much time, energy and money does one have to waste to have expectation of that change? How much damage will there be before either or both persons move on?

If the heart center is blocked, the source of pure loving energy cannot flow through and nourish the other parts of the system. You become fatigued and weighted with problems. This snowballs into self-medicating to keep the heart from feeling all the troubles. Now you are ruining your physical temple which is all you have complete control over anyway. Why would you want to destroy the house you live in every second of the day and inhibit more chance of not reaching your goals?

I suppose you are already wondering how to find your heart. Your heart is your home. It is with you at all times. How you treat it and nourish it is up to you. Fear will clog the flow of the life force provided by the heart. What can be the worst thing to happen if you face your fears? We understand fear is a natural emotion as is feeling sad or humiliated. Emotions pass eventually and it will always be your choice on how fear is accepted. It can be an adrenalin rush for some and debilitating for others. As with anything, moderation is best and learning to manage the fear is far easier than even attempting to eliminate it altogether. Our natural emotions are part of us. Fear is merely anticipation experienced before perceived danger, evil or pain appear. What is the best way to minimize the anticipation? Educate yourself on what you are fearful of doing or experiencing. The more you know the easier it is to anticipate a result comfortable for you and not for the comfort of someone else. Your heart beats at your rhythm of comfort, not another's comfort.

Chapter 28
Pearls of Wisdom

I sit here perplexed as to why this book has 28 chapters. Someone asked me how I would know when I am done. I said, "I will just know". My obsessive curiosity got the better of me as to *why 28 chapters*. So I looked for "the significance of the number 28" on the computer. Interestingly, there was an answer. Out of a myriad of explanations, the one that stood out for me was "the spiritual perfection in connection with the earth". The description of the web page also states numbers are also used in Scripture, not merely as in Nature, with the *supernatural design*, but with *spiritual significance*. Maybe I am weird for even making a connection such as this, but I followed my instinctual curiosity and found it interesting that I even found an answer to a seemingly nonsensical question. Most people would say "who cares". I always see more into something than what is there. Thank goodness, the computer does exist and the magnitude of data available is astounding.

Spiritual perfection in connection with the earth seems to say it all to me. I do not believe I have to identify this importance because anyone who has an inkling of spirituality will understand with spiritual perfection comes a perfect earth. Enlightenment of our souls, *our self*, comes when we are able to live with no fears, no insecurities, no judgments. When our heart is open and free to love all things and realize everything connects by design and significance, we will begin to start taking care of the environment. We will set in motion an understanding that spiritual perfection begets earthly perfection and if we take care of the earth, the earth will take care of us. Our crops will nourish us without fear of ecoli, our water will return to purity, animals will be able to thrive in a healthy habitat again and people will start to feel healthy again because toxins will flush from our systems and substituted with healthy food and water.

Quite a cycle I must say. Is it possible? Think about it. If you take responsibility for yourself and live life with integrity and honesty, you will have nothing to hide and your system will flow more freely. The result will be happiness for everyone concerned. If you live with deceit and lies, it will only come back and bite you in the backside to be repeated over and over until you are left with nothing but despondency and discontent. By allowing others to negatively influence the good and correct behavior that makes for positive synchronicity in the world, the world will continue to tumble into plight. If you feel you need deceit to accomplish your goals, you have some work to do on your soul level of awareness. The pain from deceit causes, in turn, magnification of the natural disasters occurring already in the world. The combined pain of all will create blocks, which manifest into physically negative fallout to the spirit and earth connection. The earth is transferring the magnified pain of humans into floods, tsunamis, hurricanes, tornadoes, and earth quakes. Yes, the earth is answering the cries of the people. This is what people are feeling.

The age of answering to your historical Karmas is coming soon and if you have not corrected the faults which karma provides for an opportunity to change, you may not be able to completely cope with the load inundated on your spirit. I am not just talking about karma from this lifetime, but from the many lifetimes you have had to correct your soul development. If you do not believe in reincarnation, then I would assume you feel you have not much to overcome. I do believe in reincarnation, and I believe some have had multiple chances to get things correct. Some things correct and adjust over time and some things remain a ball and chain around the neck. We all know what instant karma is and revel when we see it occur for others. Comments relate to an obvious malfunction of bad behavior e.g. "Hope karma comes soon for that one!" Sometimes it is easy to let go of a bad situation by knowing "karma" will eventually occur. When instant karma points to us, it tends to be surreal, but noticeable to the enlightened soul. The un-enlightened souls continue with no clue a lesson needs to exist for them.

The imprint of your past lives and foibles remain always in your center as with the pearl. It is part of you. You have choice to maintain your present way of living or you can make changes that will benefit you, and ultimately the earth and all its inhabitants.

We all have a psychic ability. The impressions of truth come as hunches, feelings, urges, visions and tingles. We have a tendency to doubt or dismiss these intimations of truth because they come so swiftly. We do not always catch the whispers because of all the clutter and racket going on around us. We live in a fast paced world that requires self-grounding and skill in recognizing when the truth emerges. This is where meditation comes in to play.

Meditation is not so difficult as we think because it only requires some alone time with the mind. If you remember, I talked about the "ranch" I frequent that totally relaxes the mind. If you cannot find the time on your own within daily activities, you may need to make the time and vacate to a quiet place. With all the chaos going on around us, finding alone time is easier said than done. I have many epiphanies in the morning when I am putting on my makeup. It is quiet in the house, I am focusing on application of the makeup and as most women know, this requires focus. It apparently leaves enough of an open window for me to hear what blows into my mind without the daily confusion of others to divert me. I have had answers come to me when I am driving alone, tuned out to people in a store while shopping, or simply taking a walk alone. This is all a form of meditation. There is no need to sit cross legged in a dark room with a candle lit if that is too time consuming for you. Of course, it would be nice to do this but our lifestyles would need a major overhaul and our neediness would necessitate controls.

The answers are within your soul already and the journey is to allow them to surface. Know the quiet answers from within your own library of data are for your personal attainment, growth and knowledge. You are already perfect and, at times, until we reach our own purity of an enlightened soul, we need reassurance this is truth. Never accept someone's truth about you if it is not positive. Absorbing their negative words only leads you to the path of doubt and hopelessness. There begins manifestation of those words into reality. The older we get, the deeper we may need to go into our psyche to find our already existing pearl.

I found a small passage written by Sri. (Swami Sivananda)

If you look in deep water only, you will find the pearl. If you keep to the shore, you will find broken shells only.

I believe these words. Take the first step. It requires faith and trust in a higher power and as Sri identifies, the treasure lies buried at the bottom of the sea. You have the capacity to dive deep within, recover the treasure and open it. Your pearl exists deep inside your heart, which is the pool of love and acceptance of your Self. If everyone takes the first step toward finding his or her unique and personal peace, the earth will begin to change and align itself with the same vibration of peace. You are the treasure. You are the pearl. My best to you on your new adventure for your Self!

ABOUT THE AUTHOR

Joanne Salsbury was born in Portsmouth, Ohio.

It is a small southern Ohio River town that is nestled in a forest area with prominent Indian heritage. She grew up knowing the land and the peace it can bring as well as the education of life beyond the books. She gained education in Europe and finalized her degrees at the University of Cincinnati.

Presently, she is living in San Diego, California where she works at a psychiatric hospital. Joanne had her own business for twelve years as a consultant in restructuring of companies with a goal of achieving high self-esteem businesses. She has done extensive public speaking and seminars for the individual as well as for companies.

Joanne is writing to all of the people in the world in hopes that each person realizes he/she can achieve high self esteem no matter of your education, circumstances or background. High self-esteem is a personal issue between you and your higher good. It is learned behavior that is compiled from all of your experiences and interactions and refined over time to paint that picture of yourself that you can love unconditionally.

Our natural emotions have been distorted in value over time and she would like to help you remember and gain back the understanding and purpose of your own emotions, so you can have your own self esteem back as well.

www.ingramcontent.com/pod-product-compliance
Lightning Source LLC
Chambersburg PA
CBHW061142040426
42445CB00013B/1513